THE BIG
BOOK
OF DRAWING

THE BIG BOOK OF DRAWING

The history, study, materials,
techniques, subjects, theory,
and practice of artistic drawing
by

JOSÉ M. PARRAMÓN

WATSON - GUPTILL PUBLICATIONS / NEW YORK

Published 1987 in Spain by Parramón Ediciones, S.A., Barcelona

First published 1987 in the United States by Watson-Guptill Publications,
a division of Billboard Publications, Inc.
1515 Broadway, New York, N.Y. 10036

Library of Congress Cataloging-in-Publication Data
Parramón, José María
The big book of drawing.
Translation of: El gran libro del dibujo.
1. Drawing-Technique. I. Title.
NC735.P37 1987   741.2   86-28279
ISBN: 0-8230-0497-X

Manufactured in Spain by Graficromo, S.A.
Polígono Las Quemadas - Córdoba
Legal deposit: CO-1720-87

1

Contents

To Carmen, Mercedes, and José María

Fig. 3. Francesc Serra. (1912-1976). *Study of a Head*. Blue chalk highlighted with white chalk on cream paper. Private collection.

3

introduction

Before beginning a painting, the great masters of the past drew and then painted several preliminary versions. This is still done nowadays. The old masters also began their works with *painted drawings.* First they gave the canvas or the piece of wood a coat of glue and plaster. Some artists dyed or repainted this mixture: Titian and Velázquez with reddish-sienna, Rubens with silver-gray. They would then paint on top of that coat with one or two colors and white. Rubens, for example, after adding a coat of silver-gray tone, would draw in the model with a dark ochre, and later enhance light areas with white. Eventually, taking this painted drawing as a starting point, Rubens would complete the painting using all the colors of his palette.

John Sloan, a founding member of the Ash Can School (famous for its paintings of sordid slums in New York), wrote a book detailing his ideas on art. He stated, "The great painters used to separate shape and color. Firstly, they used to paint shapes with neutral colors by drawing them. Then, they added color." Sloan also states that:

Painting is drawing.

Indeed, when we paint, we are drawing. When painting a tree, the artist must first draw–with paint–its length and thickness, its illuminated and shadowed areas. Many other artists have remarked, as Ingres did, "We paint the same as we draw."

The purpose of this book is to teach the art of drawing, both as an end in itself and as part of the process of painting.

The book begins with a summary of the history of artistic drawing. To illuminate this summary are reproductions of works by Leonardo, Michelangelo, Raphael, Rubens, Watteau, and other master draftsmen. Various media are discussed, such as colored pencils, oil crayons, oil pastels, chalk pastels, and even watercolor. You may wonder why so many media are included in a book about drawing. They are here because they can be used for both painting *and* drawing; thus they provide an important link between the two art forms.

In discussing drawing materials, I have tried to remain impartial regarding brands and manufacturers. After each presentation, I have commented on the use and techniques of the various materials. Keep in mind that the basic principles of perspective, proportions, light and shade, value contrasts, composition, form and space can be applied to both drawing and painting. However, in this book we have chosen drawings as examples.

4

Fig. 4. Peter Paul Rubens (1577-1640). *The Annunciation.* Ashmolean Museum, Oxford. Rubens began this first stage of the panel by painting in a layer of silver-gray color, then drawing the model with touches of ochre, and finally working the light areas with white paint.

introduction

Finally, I have stressed throughout the book the necessity of drawing as much as possible, of finding models and subjects everywhere, and knowing there are tools and techniques to achieve real masterpieces. Practice–steadfast work at your drawing–is the most important factor in learning to draw. Matisse proclaimed, "We must work as workmen. He who has done something worthwhile has worked in this way." Working also means thinking; "having the picture in our mind" (Monet), or walking along a street "keeping our mind busy, observing men's and women's faces on cloudy days" (Leonardo). Making good use of your time is also important: "Everybody is amazed at how much I paint. But the point is that instead of wandering to and fro, like many other artists I know do, I shut myself in my studio" (Delacroix). Geneviève Laporte, one of the women in Picasso's life, wrote a book called *Picasso's Secret Love*, in which she presents Picasso's ideas and attitudes while he was with her. "We used to talk about the young artists: 'Young artists think it is enough to do what I used to do at their age: chatting, drinking, smoking, going to cafes . . . and wait for fame and success to arrive.' He sent out a puff of smoke and half-closing his eyes he said: "That's not true. You have to *work*.'"

José M. Parramón

5

6

Figs. 5 and 6. The art of drawing offers many possibilities, not only because of the variety of themes, for example, portraits, landscapes, and still life; but also because of the different media, for example, charcoal, Conté, pastels, and colored pencil. In the drawings at left, you can see examples of this diversity: the black and white rendering of the head of a young girl drawn in lead pencil of an HB grade on fine grain paper, and the cactus drawing made with oil crayons.

Fig. 7. Maurice Quentin de La Tour (1704-1788). *Self-portrait*. Louvre, Paris.

history
of the art
# of drawing

The simplest essay produced by the hand of
an artist will enhance the theory of art more
than a million volumes.

Sir Joshua Reynolds (1723-1792)

20,000 years b.c.

At the beginning of this century, the German ethnologist Leo Frobenius noticed that "to hunt a deer, the aboriginals of a tribe drew the effigy of the animal on a rock, then threw their arrows at it, and only after that did they set off to capture it."

Frobenius and most ethnologists agree that this behavior was not an isolated practice. More than 20,000 years ago Paleolithic men drew animals on the walls of the caves they lived in. The purpose of these drawings was to request the gods' help when fishing and hunting.

Those men were the first artists acknowledged as such. They drew large figures. They preferred hard rock walls where they engraved the animals' profiles with flint chisels. They outlined the animals with coal, and colored the surface with earthen pigments of various shades: black, brown, yellow, and rarely, purple. They used blood, fat, and vegetable resins to bind the colors.

Those people were nomadic and basically naturalistic, therefore their painting were completely realistic. It was not until the Neolithic period, thousands of years later, that men learned to cultivate land, build dwellings, domesticate animals, establish economic systems, and set up villages and towns. The Neolithic period also brought the use of geometry and shapes, and saw a rejection of much of the naturalism of Paleolithic man. Neolithic art consisted mainly of abstract embellishments on utensils, vessels, tools, and weapons. It was not until 3,200 B.C. that the relay was taken up again. It was then that the history of ancient Egypt began.

Egypt: Art of the Pharaohs and Eternal Life

In ancient Egypt, the king, or pharaoh, was regarded as a god. Both pharaoh and subjects believed in immortality. Thus, Egyptian art was always directed by pharaoh and was meant for the life that was to continue beyond death. All ancient Egyptian paintings, whether they were murals or on papyrus, can be found in tombs. They all depict what the dead person and his life and surroundings were like. This kind of message picture was sketched first on limestone boards called *ostraca*. From those, the artist would carry out the final work on a wall or a wooden board previously covered with a coat of stucco made of white lime.

Egyptian artists used fine brushes made with rushes crushed at one end and red color made of iron oxide agglutinated with gum arabic and egg white. Having drawn the outline, they colored the shapes in plain colors, without regard for light and shade effects.

Fig. 8. *Bison.* Altamira Caves, Spain.

Fig. 9. *Bison Carved on a Reindeer's Horn.* Madelaine's Grotto. Museum of St. Germain-en-Laye, France. 13,000 years ago men were already capable of drawing the contours and forms of animals with great style.

egypt: art of the pharaohs and eternal life

10

Fig. 10. New Empire, mural painting of the School of Thebes, *Egyptian Dancers*. British Museum, London. Egyptian art is subject to a series of traditional forms: In the human figure, faces are inexpressive, the features are impersonal and the head and the legs are in profile while the torso is drawn as seen from the front. From the beginnings of Egyptian art, female bodies are painted ochre-yellow and the male bodies red. Curiously, these artistic conventionalities do not happen in animal drawings, which are more lifelike, painted in a variety of colors.

11

Fig. 11. *Inspection of the Cattle*. Detail of Nebamon's tomb. School of Thebes. British Museum, London. Egyptian art is subject to a series of traditional formulas: The features of the face are inexpressive; the head and legs are always seen in profile while the chest is drawn frontally. (This rule is constant with very few exceptions, such as the dancer above in Fig. 10.) From the beginning of Egyptian art, female bodies are painted in yellow ochre, male bodies in red ochre. It is curious that these color conventions do not exist in animal drawings, where varied colors create the forms.

the greeks (776 b.c.)

In 776 B.C., when the first Olympic Games took place, the Greeks began to record and write their history. The chroniclers of that period: Pausanias, Plutarch, and Aristotle among the Greeks, and Pliny Herodotus, and others among the Romans, tell us about the great Greek artists and draftsmen. They mention Polygnotus as one of the great masters who painted murals and started up a school. They also refer to the prominent sculptor Phidias, who was the first disciple of Polygnotus and who copied the figures of his master to create his own sculptures for the Parthenon. They tell about Zeuxis, who painted with such realism that on one occasion birds came up to peck at the grapes he had painted. They write of the artist Apelles, renowned for his great skill, who was chosen by Alexander the Great as his only portraitist. The Roman historian Pliny, in Volume 35 of his *Natural History*, where he deals with ancient art, records that Parrhasio's disciples learned to draw using silver or lead tips on parchment or wooden boards covered with bone dust. This technique, metalpoint, is exactly the same one described by Cennino Cennini and used by Pisanello in Italy a thousand years later.

Fig. 12 (above). Attributed to Onesimos. *Girl Preparing to Take a Bath.* 480 B.C. Royal Museum of Art and History, Brussels.

Fig. 13. Euphronius, painter, and Euxitheos, ceramist. *Dream and Death Lifting the Body of King Sarpedon.* Metropolitan Museum of Art, New York.

13   14

Fig. 14. Exekias, painter and ceramist. *Achilles Killing Penthesileia* (Queen of the Amazons). British Museum, London.

Unfortunately, there are no existing studies, pictures, or murals drawn and painted by the great masters of ancient Greece. However, Greek pottery and Roman painting–copied from Greek painting–does confirm the existence and high quality of the works mentioned by Greek and Roman historians.

In fact, the figures, subjects, and scenes found in Greek pottery were very often based on those depicted in wall paintings, as many artists were both painters and potters. The quality of the images, particularly those drawn on certain funeral vases called *lekythoi*, shows that the art of drawing flourished in ancient Greece.

On the other hand, it is widely accepted that the majority of Roman paintings found at Pompeii, Herculaneum, and other places are copies, albeit bad copies, of Greek paintings. For example, the mosaic found at Pompeii of the Battle of Issus, in which Alexander the Great is shown fighting Darius of Persia, may be a copy of a famous painting by Apelles' disciple Philoxenus from the fourth century B.C.

Fig. 15. Painter of Penthesileia. *The Judgment of Paris.* Ceramic. A vessel for keeping cosmetics. 460 B.C. Metropolitan Museum of Art, New York.

Fig. 16. Reed painter; a lekythos, or funerary vessel. National Museum, Athens.

Fig. 17. *Quiron Instructs Young Achilles.* A mural found in Herculaneum; possibly a copy of an original by Apelles. National Museum, Naples.

Fig. 18. Mosaic copy of a painting by Apelles and his pupil Philoxenos, *The Battle of Issus.* Mosaic found in the House of the Faun, Pompeii. National Museum, Naples.

rome

From its very beginning, Roman art was a reflection of Greek art. It began in the sixth century B.C. in Etruria, in the center of Italy. It reached maturity in the third century B.C., when Rome ruled over central Italy and had spread its influence to Greek towns in the south of Italy. The treasures of Greek art were then taken to Italy, where Romans became passionate collectors.

The development that drawing and painting had achieved in Rome can be seen in the ornamentation of houses and buildings at Pompeii and Herculaneum. Both cities were buried during the eruption of Vesuvius in A.D. 79. The wall paintings from Pompeii show Roman art with basically ornamental themes and style, and frescoes copied from Greek wall paintings.

Besides themes, style, and clothing, there is something that proves Roman painting was highly influenced by Greece: The Greek and Roman chroniclers mention more than fifty Greek painters and draftsmen. The only Roman artist mentioned by Roman historians is Fabius Pictor. One important reason for the lack of recognition Roman artists received is that art was seen primarily as a way of glorifying the lives and deeds of the emperors and was not generally favored for its own sake. In Augustus' days there are more than eighty statues with his effigy just in the city of Rome itself: Augustus the young child, Augustus the valiant warrior, Augustus the benevolent patrician, Augustus the mighty emperor.

19

Fig. 19. Anonymous. *Portrait.* First half of the second century B.C. National Gallery, London. Greek and Roman artists, established in Fayun, Upper Egypt, during the Roman Empire, painted portraits similar to this one. These portraits were encaustic paintings (hot waxes mixed with pigments) painted on wood, made for the frontispieces of the sarcophagi that contained the mummies of the portrayed.

Figs. 20 and 21. (above) Wall painting from the House of Livia, in the Palatine, Rome. (below) Wall painting from the House of the Vetii, Pompeii. In Roman painting proper, there were four different styles: The first is called the *incrustation* style, which shows the complex ornamentation of the moldings, doors, windows, and pilasters. The second style, called *architectonic*, reproduces the effects of perspective and depth (see foreground in the figure above) and mixed, at times, with natural subjects. The third style, the *ornamental*, is mainly decorative. And the fourth, the *illusionist* style (left), is a mixture of the other three, with effects of perspective and depth, encrusted moldings, frames, and, as seen in the central area, a copy of a Greek painting.

21

indian and islamic art

Indian art from the third century B.C. was mainly Buddhist art. It was also the art of sculpture. Until A.D. 800, Hindu architects and sculptors built temples and shrines with plenty of sculptures. Many of these temples were carved in rock cliffs.

Among these buildings, nearly thirty caves carved in Ajanta, in central India, must be mentioned. Besides sculptures and bas-reliefs, there is a series of wall paintings considered among the greatest masterpieces ever made by man. The outstanding quality of these frescoes made them into models not only for artists who painted murals many years after, but even for manuscript illustrators.

In the Middle Ages, artists in India drew on palm leaves, which necessitated a long and narrow format. They marked the surface with metalpoint, a primitive pencil. Then they scattered dark blue dust on the surface and blew it off in order to get the drawing. In the fourteenth century, paper was introduced in India. It came from Persia and helped in the making of drawings and miniatures which, from then on, were to be painted with watercolors and opaque colors (gouache).

In 622 Mohammed left Mecca and went to Yathrib (now Medina), Saudi Arabia, and founded a new religion: Islam. A hundred years later the Islamic world was an empire that covered a vast territory, from Tibet to the Atlantic Ocean and included all the peoples and nations of the southern coast of the Mediterranean.

The Koran, the holy book of Islam, does not ban the representation of images in art. However, the ancient Muslim theologians pontificated that drawing people implied a sinful arrogation of the divine power of creation and doing so was banned in religious books and buildings. Islamic artists then developed all sorts of decorative embellishments until the Koran was revised and no reason could be found for the previous ban.

In the fourteenth century, Tamerlane, heading the Mongolians, went as far as Turkey and India and established the first Timurid school of miniaturists in Persia. Persia then became the artistic center of Islamic art. Among others the schools of Herat and Mugal of Akbar were established at this time; and artists such as Bihzad, Aqa Riza, and Riza i'Abbasi were working during this fertile period. Riza i'Abbasi was the most prominent Islamic draftsman and painter, and also the founder of the Abbasi school.

22

Fig. 22. Mughal School of Akbar. *Zanbur, the Spy* Metropolitan Museum of Art, New York. The original of this page of the manuscript measures 29 1/2″ x 22 1/2″ (74 x 57.2 cm). It was painted with watercolors, opaque colors, and gold on cotton cloth mounted on paper. It belongs to a series of fourteen volumes, each one including a hundred illustrations similar to this one. Note that the high perspective point gives a good illumination of the facts of the scene. The laborious ornamentation of houses and mansions is characteristic of Islamic art.

Fig. 23. Anonymous. *Balkis, Queen of Sheba*, (fragment). British Museum, London. The subject, the Queen of Sheba and her love affair with Solomon, has been represented by such well-known artists as Raphael, Veronese, and Claude Lorrain.

23

far east: china and japan

The Chinese use the same materials for both writing and paintings; that is, silk or paper, ink, and a brush. "All colors are possible in ink," the Chinese say, although when painting, they also use watercolors.

This has been true for centuries. However, there have always been two classic styles of expression in Chinese art: the linear and the tonal. The linear is based on sketches made with a brush. Outlines and inner lines are drawn on white backgrounds, and images are painted with plain colors without any shading or relief. The tonal style is based on shades of color rather than on lines. This style, developed in the Han age (206 B.C.-A.D. 221), helped solve the needs of landscape painting and, as a consequence, gave rise to the invention of paper and the further development of brushes.

Calligraphy and drawing became closely related during the Han period. Artists used to say a painting is a poem without words. Poems and sentences were written on the same scrolls as landscapes, the favorite subject in Chinese art. These landscapes were composed of tints, contrasts, and subtle tonal gradations that suggest mood and pictorial depth.

Among the best representatives of the linear style were Yen Li-pen (seventh century) and Fan K'uan (twelfth century). Good examples of the tonal tendency were Wang Wei (eighth century) and Mu Ch'i (thirteenth century).

In Japanese art, the traditional media were watercolors and gouache. At first, Japanese art was a reflection of Buddhism and Chinese art. But by the tenth century new subjects were introduced, and a pure Japanese style appeared. It was the so-called Yamato-e style. During the Kamakura period, subjects became more dramatic. With the advent of Zen, priests, and particularly a monk called Sesshu, introduced simple subjects and the use of monochromatic wash. Those styles were cultivated by the Kano school derived from the Sumi-e and the Tosa schools, which monopolized the national Yamato-e style.

In 1683, Hishikawa Moronobu printed an engraving with a nonreligious subject. The idea was successful, and in the eighteenth and nineteenth centuries, plates with Japanese engravings reached Paris, where they influenced the Impressionists and spread all over the world. This new way of expression was followed by many Japanese artists, most notably Harunobu, Utamaro, and Hokusai.

Fig. 24. Kuo Hsi. *Chinese Wintry Landscape* (detail). Eleventh century. Museum of Art, Toledo, Ohio. Traditional example of a Chinese landscape showing the characteristic tonal subtleties, blendings, light and shade effects, and spatial illusion.

Fig. 25. Ando Hiroshige (1797-1858). *Flowers and Birds.* Hermitage, Leningrad.

Fig. 26. Katsushika Hokusai (1760-1849). *Birds in Flight*. Uffizi, Florence. Hokusai lived for 89 years. He is attributed with about 30.000 works, including paintings, engravings, and drawings. His most famous collection is the *mangwa* (meaning copious drawings), consisting of fifteen volumes that represent the character of people in action, from the elegant bourgeois to the most humble worker, their tools and clothes, and the streets and houses of everyday life. His work influenced artists from the West, especially the Impressionists Degas, Van Gogh, and Toulouse-Lautrec. In this drawing on white Japanese paper, painted with a wash of India ink and ochre-yellow watercolor, Hokusai shows us his extraordinary imagination and memory, as well as his clever handling of composition.

medieval art in europe

In the fourth century, Rome ruled over two vast territories: the western Roman Empire and the eastern Roman Empire. In the latter, Rome had to create a new center of power because of the recurrent wars and the pressures exerted by the barbarians. Thus, the Roman Emperor Constantine the Great chose the former Byzantium to found Constantinople, the capital of the new Byzantine Empire.

More than a hundred years later, the barbarians sacked Rome. The Roman Catholic Church was the only institution that managed to escape the cataclysm. Helped by Eastern and Western rulers, the church condemned classical art and promoted Christian art as a means of spreading the religion.

In Byzantium, art became theological. The images of Jesus, the Virgin, and the saints appear in mosaics, though not in paintings, and are shown richly dressed to imitate the hieratic and authoritarian ritual of the court. Then, in the year 726, the Iconoclast movement began its attempt to suppress the sensuousness of the classical period. All figurative representations were forbidden and sculptures and paintings of images were destroyed. "Churches remained entirely white, and those who dared sculpt or paint were severely punished," wrote the sculptor Ghiberti in the fifteenth century. After this period, a renaissance of art began in Byzantium, which, in drawing and painting, produced parchments and miniatures in the ancient classical style such as the *Psalter of Paris*.

In the meantime, the West had been invaded by the barbarians. The historian Arnold Hauser wrote about this age of decay, "During the sixth and seventh centuries no one in the West was able to draw a human figure." After this dark period, we find Charlemagne, who founded the Carolingian Empire in the ninth century. Before the year 800 there was already a famous Irish school of miniaturists, among whose works is the *Book of Kells*. Charlemagne attracted artists of this school, as well as Italian and English artists such as Alcuin. He also stimulated a cultural renaissance of a religious kind and established the *scriptoria* at Fulda, Luxeuil, and Tours. The study of metrics and grammar was given emphasis as well. As a result of these changes, Romanesque art appeared. However, when the Carolingian Empire lost its strength as a state, and the power of lords, barons, and courts was acknowledged, feudalism emerged. Feudalism divided Europe into hundreds of small states, each one closed to the rest and isolated from the world. In the long run, this hindered the development of art and culture.

In the twelfth century, the Gothic period in art began. Life came back to cities, and art experienced a new awakening. In Italy, Giotto became a successful artist in the thirteenth century. In France, the Villard de Honnecourt compiled hundreds of sketches in a "lodge book", or sketchbook, as we would say today. He collected plans of buildings, figure studies, animal studies, and war machines.

In 1150 paper began to be produced in Spain, and by the fourteenth century throughout Europe. During the 1390s the artist and educator Cennino Cennini wrote his famous book *Il Libro dell'Arte*. There, he dealt with the techniques of artistic drawing and enumerated the tools and materials needed, from the metalpoint (primitive pencil) to colored papers.

In the fifteenth century, when drawing began to be considered an art in itself, Pisanello became a prominent figure of the international Gothic style. Many of his sketches and drawings are included in the Vallardi Codex, one of the best collections of drawings of that period. There we can find studies of animals, clothes, and antiques, and sketches of paintings, including nudes, drawn with a metalpoint on white drawing paper tinted with pale colors. The Renaissance had come at last, and the art of drawing had established itself once and for all.

Figs. 27 and 28. (below) Pisanello (1395-1455). *Woman's Head, Study.* Louvre, Paris. (left) *Head of a Woman Turned to the Left in Profile.* Pellegrini Chapel of Saint Anastasia, Verona. This detail of a woman's head, done in ink with a pen over black chalk, was a preliminary study for a fresco.

Fig. 29. Simone Martini (1284-1344). *Blessing Christ with the Angels.* Papal Palace, Avignon. Charcoal underpainting for a fresco mural.

Fig. 30. Anonymous Irish illustrator (A.D. 800). *Book of Kells* (initial). Trinity College Library, Dublin. The *Book of Kells*, 15 x 10 in. (33 x 25 cm), is tempera painted on parchment. It is the most important manuscript of the Irish school, noted for the originality and beauty of its miniatures.

Fig. 31. Lorenzo Monaco (1370/2-1425). *Mary's Meeting with Elisabeth* Dahlem Museum, Berlin. Lorenzo Monaco, also called Lorenzo the Monk, was a "modern" artist of his time. He introduced the International Gothic style into Florence, by changing the golden backgrounds and flat figures of traditional Gothic art to more realistic details. The backgrounds become landscapes, and figures have depth, an idea that was later adopted by Ghiberti, Martini, and Pisanello. The originality of Lorenzo Monaco is evident in this pen and ink and tempera drawing on parchment.

27

28

Fig. 32. Anonymous. *Joshua Receiving the Emissaries.* Vatican Museum, Rome. The biblical character Joshua is represented here, by a Byzantine artist of the tenth century, in a *volume* (parchment scroll rolled up on a wood cylinder) drawn in pen and ink and wash.

29

30

31

32

Making Paper

Around the year A.D. 105, the Chinese Minister of Agriculture developed the process of manufacturing paper. This invention did not reach the West until the year 751, when the Chinese were defeated by the Arabs in the Battle of Talas (in Russia near the Chinese border). Some experts in paper manufacturing were captured, and later, paper factories were set up in the Middle East and Northern Africa.

Eventually, paper making was brought to Europe, first to the Iberian Peninsula: Córdoba (1040), Játiva, and Catalonia (1150). Later, factories were built in Italy (1276), France (1348), Germany (1390), and elsewhere. By 1390, when the artist and educator Cennino Cennini wrote his well-known book *Il Libro dell'Arte,* in which he describes the techniques of artistic drawing complete with the tools and materials needed, he included colored papers. Around 1740, James Whatman in England made the first watercolor paper; one hundred years later, Etienne Carson in France developed a new method of sizing paper, which resulted in Canson drawing paper, a well-known high quality paper still available today.

33

Fig. 33. The raw materials used to make paper are wood, vegetable fibers, old paper, and cotton rags. These materials, first sorted, cut up, and sized, become what is called stuff, which is the basis of paper making, and consists mainly of cellulose.

34

Fig. 34. To make a sheet of paper, use a frame with a wire mesh. The amount of stuff necessary for one sheet is spread over the mesh.

35

Fig. 35. Once the water has drained from the sheet and it begins to stiffen, it is removed and covered with a piece of felt on top and a piece of fine smooth cloth underneath.

Fig. 36. Next, a number of sheets complete with their pieces of felt and cloth are put in a press so that any remaining water will be pressed out. As a final step, the sheets are dried and prepared for either a rough or smooth surface.

the renaissance: the quattrocento

The pioneers of the Renaissance were three artists from Florence: the painter Masaccio, the sculptor Donatello, and the architect Brunelleschi. They knew each other's work and together they created a new type of art. After them, in about a century's time, the greatest masters of drawing and painting ever known appeared: Botticelli, Leonardo da Vinci, Michelangelo, Raphael, Titian, and Correggio. When talking about the fifteenth century, or Quattrocento, there is a family name that stands out: Bellini. The father, Jacopo, produced two books of sketches which inspired his sons Gentile and Giovanni. Giovanni followed his father's guidelines and became the most prominent master of his generation. Other artists who lived and worked at the time are Botticelli (probably a disciple of Fra Filippo Lippi), Paolo Ucello, Piero della Francesca (who improved the theories of perspective developed by Brunelleschi) and Verrocchio (master of

37

38

39

40

Fig. 37. Jacopo Bellini (1400-1470). *A Saint Preaching in a Town.* Ink and wash parchment. Louvre, Paris.

Fig. 38. Filippino Lippi (1457-1504). *Study for a Figure in Action.* Charcoal or sanguine, highlighted with white chalk on pink-tinted paper. Uffizi Gallery, Florence.

Fig. 39. Sandro Botticelli (1445-1510). *Abundance, or Autumn.* Black chalk, sepia watercolor, sepia ink, and white chalk highlights on pink-tinted paper. British Museum, London.

Fig. 40. Andrea del Verrochio (1435-1488). *Woman's Head with a Complicated Hairstyle.* Black charcoal highlighted with opaque white (tempera/gouache), Metropolitan Museum, New York.

Leonardo) also lived and worked at this time. There are other masters in the Quattrocento who should be mentioned. Antonello da Messina who was influenced by the Flemish master Jan Van Eyck; Rogier van der Weyden, also Flemish; Hans Memling, from Germany; François Fouquet from France; Jaume Huguet from Catalonia; and Gentile da Fabriano, Andrea Mantegna, Domenico Ghirlandaio, and Perugino from Italy.

By the time of the Renaissance, drawing was already a compulsory subject for the artist. It can be said that to paint well, one must draw better. Artists were already using the means present-day artists have, that is, white and colored papers, the metalpoints, charcoal, sanguine, brushes, watercolor, and gouache.

Fig. 41. Antonello da Messina (1430-1479). *Portrait of a Boy.* Charcoal on sepia-tinted paper. Albertina Museum, Vienna.

Fig. 42. Lorenzo di Credi (1459-1537). *Head of a Youth with Long Hair.* Drawing made with metalpoint on yellow-tinted paper. Albertina Museum, Vienna.

41

Metalpoint

According to Pliny in 400 B.C., the pupils of the Greek painter Parrhasios already drew with a metalpoint, a handle with a tip on one end. This tip was made of lead, silver, or gold. Its marks were black but on a prepared ground left an impression similar to our present-day lead pencil, though a bit lighter. Parrhasio's pupils drew on parchment or wooden boards prepared with bone dust and gum arabic.

Cennino Cennini, author of *Il Libro dell'Arte* (1390), mentions the metalpoint, also called a stylus, and describes the preparation of the surface with chalk dust and saliva. This procedure was commonplace and was used in the fifteenth and sixteenth centuries by most Dutch, Italian, and German artists.

If you want to try this technique, a plumber can provide you with a 4 in. (10 cm) pencil-shaped piece of lead or solder. Sharpen this tip with a pencil sharpener and you will be able to draw, preferably on couché (laid) paper, with the same tool used 500 years ago by Giotto, Botticelli, Leonardo da Vinci, Michelangelo, Raphael, and Dürer.

43

42

leonardo da vinci

Leonardo da Vinci was a genius; he was not simply an artist, but also excelled as a sculptor, an architect, an urbanist, a physicist, a botanist, a biologist, an artillery designer, a mechanic, an anatomist, a geologist, a writer, and a poet. Before airplanes were invented, he thought of the parachute; he also proposed a theory of gravity two hundred years before Newton's law. He was one of the foremost pioneers in the field of comparative anatomy. He is known to have developed more than thirty inventions, among them, the steam pump, the howitzer, the hand grenade, and the darkroom.

But Leonardo was mainly a painter and a draftsman. In his *Treatise on Painting* (which has been translated into most languages), he provided timeless observations on drawing, such as his assertion in the chapter entitled "Drawing: Outlines and Reliefs": "The closer the outlines of a figure are to our eyes, the sharper and lighter they appear."

Leonardo drew anything that motivated his imagination and intelligence: plans and sketches of his inventions, studies of figures both still and in motion, intricate botanical illustrations, landscape and figure sketches, studies of poses and facial expressions, caricatures, and self-portraits. He drew for the sake of drawing and made use of all materials and techniques known at that time. It is also well known that he loved preparing new colors, developing new binding media, new solvents, and varnishes.

Leonardo drew on papers tinged with blue, green, ochre, yellow, cream, or pink, using crayon or pen with inks of various colors. He also combined media, for example, crayon, charcoal, and metalpoint. He paid great attention to tones, chiaroscuro, and *sfumato,* which he did with his fingers. He improved upon the "hard and dry style" (as the great art historian Vasari called it) of the Quattrocento. His interpretation of contrast, space, and atmosphere looks very modern, and he never fell into affectation.

Leonardo, though he belonged to the generation before Michelangelo and Raphael, was truly one of the three great creators of the High Renaissance.

44

46

45

Fig. 44. (top) Leonardo da Vinci (1452-1519). *Study for Virgin of the Rocks.* National Library, Turin.

Fig. 45. (above) *Virgin of the Rocks* (detail). Louvre, Paris. The structure of the face and its subtle value gradations make this an example of a perfectly finished drawing.

Fig. 46. (left) Leonardo da Vinci, *Virgin with Saint Anne,* Royal Academy of Art, London.

Fig. 47. Leonardo da Vinci. *Woman's Head*. Uffizi Gallery, Florence.

Fig. 48. Leonardo da Vinci. *Madonna and Child with a Cat*. Ink on paper. British Museum, London.

Fig. 49. (right). Leonardo da Vinci. *Self-portrait*. Sanguine. Metropolitan Museum of Art, New York.

michelangelo

One of the great challenges for fifteenth century sculptors was making the pyramidal composition of the dead Jesus stretched almost horizontally in the lap of his mother Mary. Michelangelo Buonarotti managed to accomplish it when he was only twenty-three. The *Pietà* in Saint Peter's, Rome, is the most sublime composition of the death of Jesus Christ. Seventeen years later, at the age of thirty-five, he finished the ceiling of the Sistine Chapel, the greatest wall painting of all time, "with three hundred square meters and 343 figures" (Papini). Michelangelo was also an architect and was in charge of the work at Saint Peter's Basilica in Rome, its dome being his personal masterpiece.

Like many Renaissance artists, Michelangelo was a poet. He was a prolific draftsman as well. About five hundred of his drawings, most of them studies of figures for wall paintings or pictures, have been preserved. Some of these drawings are only sketches, but others are entirely finished. Some of them are made with charcoal, others with crayon. They were done on ochre or cream paper with highlights in white chalk.

Before he died, Michelangelo had the opportunity to read his own biography. Written by the art historian Vasari, it stated that he was the greatest of all sculptors, painters, and draftsmen and one of the best architects and poets. It is a curious fact that while he was painting the Sistine ceiling, Michelangelo abhorred his recognition as a painter since he regarded himself primarily as a sculptor. To his friend Giovanni da Pistoia he said: "Giovanni, defend my dead painting and my honor as an artist for . . . I am no painter."

50

51

Fig. 50. Michelangelo (1475-1564). *Studies for the Libyan Sibyl* (detail). Sanguine on yellow paper. Metropolitan Museum of Art, New York.

Fig. 51. *The Libyan Sibyl.* Fresco on a wall of the Sistine Chapel. Vatican, Rome.

Fig. 52. *Soul of a Convicted Person.* Charcoal. Uffizi Gallery, Florence.

Fig. 53. Michelangelo. *Naked Man Sitting*. Sanguine drawing highlighted with white chalk. Albertina Museum, Vienna. The study of the Sibyl (opposite page) and this one of a man sitting are two excellent examples of the artistic abilities of Michelangelo in every aspect of drawing: the perfect construction of the form, proportions, and dimensions; the subtle gradations of tone, the precision of the highlighted areas, and a perfect resolution of the shaded area setting off the chiaroscuro effects, the light on the shade. There is also a masterful lesson on anatomy to be found here. Anatomy was a subject unknown in those times; Michelangelo studied it for himself by going to the morgue at Holy Ghost Hospital in Florence, where he would work secretly by the light of an oil lamp. In those times, the dissection of a corpse, even for scientific study, was completely forbidden and prosecuted with a prison penalty.

53

raphael

Raphael was born in Urbino, Italy, on April 6, 1483. His mother died when he was eight and his father when Raphael was eleven. We do not known much about him until he was seventeen, when we find him working in Perugino's workshop. He then signed his first contract to paint *The Coronation of the Blessed Nicolas of Tolentino*. At nineteen he painted *The Coronation of the Holy Virgin* and at twenty-one, *The Marriage of the Virgin*, which was admired by all his contemporaries, even Perugino.

Pope Julius II called on Raphael at the age of twenty-five (1508), to decorate the walls of the *Stanza*, the rooms at the Vatican with wall paintings. Perugino, Bramantino, and Sodoma were already working on these rooms. The Pope entrusted the first room, la Stanza della Segnatura, to Raphael. But no sooner did he see the first sketches than the Pope gave all the rooms to him, "dismissing the rest and their stories," according to Vasari. By then Michelangelo was thirty-three and had already begun the ceiling of the Sistine Chapel. Michelangelo and Raphael were the only artists employed by the Vatican. Six years later, Raphael succeeded Bramante as the architect of Saint Peter's. Raphael was clever; he organized a workshop with many good disciples to help him with his assignments from the Pope, kings, and princes who asked for pictures, wall paintings, and tapestries. To carry out these assignments he used his own studies, sketches, and drawings. What a pity that he died at thirty-seven.

Fig. 54 (below, left). Raphael (1483-1520). *Study of Naked Men*. Preliminary drawing. Metalpoint and sanguine on white paper. Albertina Museum, Vienna. Raphael's level of craftsmanship and aesthetic quality make him a master of classical drawing.

Figs. 55 and 56 (above). *Study for Venus and Psyche*. Sanguine. Louvre, Paris. (Left) School of Raphael, *Venus and Psyche*. Farnesina, Rome.

Figs. 57 and 58 (left). *Study for Saint Catherine of Alexandria.* Charcoal drawing and white chalk on white paper. Louvre, Paris. (Below) *Saint Catherine of Alexandria.* National Gallery, London.

Fig. 59 (right). *Woman Reading to a Child.* Metalpoint and white chalk on gray-tinted paper. Devonshire Collection, Chatsworth, England.

Fig. 60. *Cartoon for the School of Athens.* Sienna watercolor. Ambrosian Art Gallery, Milan.

58

59

60

the cinquecento: florence and rome

Lorenzo the Magnificent was known as a prince and a banker but also as a poet, philosopher, and a patron of the arts. His death in Florence in 1492, followed by the exile of his family, the Medicis, and Savonarola's dictatorship, displaced Florence as the cultural center of Italy. It was replaced by Rome, where the patronage of Pope Julius II and the fame of the Vatican sculptures and paintings was spreading among Italian artists.

The Renaissance had begun in Florence. After Brunelleschi, Masaccio, and Donatello, the Florentines recognized Leonardo and Verrocchio as great artists. Leonardo, who studied at Verrocchio's workshop, produced such a great work in *The Baptism* that his master gave up painting. Andrea del Sarto, Pontormo, Rosso, and Bronzino were also Florentines. Together with Tintoretto (Venice) and Parmigianino (Parma), they started the Mannerist movement, which flourished between the Renaissance and the Baroque periods.

Rome was at that time (1500—1525) the leading capital of the Renaissance. Michelangelo and Raphael were carrying out the most representative sculptures and paintings of the age. Pope Julius II was a wholehearted lover of art. Many prominent Florentine artists in addition to Michelangelo and Raphael, and some others from Venice and Parma, met in Rome and spent time there drawing, painting, and sculpting. Even Leonardo lived in Rome between 1513 and 1516. They were all great draftsmen who valued drawing as an independent art.

Fig. 63 (right). Jacopo Carrucci Pontormo (1494-1557). Detail of *Three Men Walking, Study.* Sanguine. Museum of Fine Arts, Lille, France.

Fig. 64 (right, above). Correggio, Antonio Allegri (c. 1490-1534). *Eve.* Sanguine and white chalk. Louvre, Paris.

Fig. 65 (right, below). Francesco Massuoli Parmigianino (1503-1540). *Study of a Caryatid.* Preliminary drawing of metal point, sanguine, and white chalk on cream paper. Albertina Museum, Vienna.

Fig. 61. Andrea del Sarto (1486-1531). *Head of an Old Man.* Charcoal. Uffizi Gallery, Florence.

Fig. 62. Federico Barocci (1528-1615). *Study of the Head of an Old Man.* Black chalk, sanguine, and white chalk on gray-green tinted paper. Hermitage, Leningrad.

61

62

the cinquecento: venice

Titian, the great Venetian artist, painted his pictures without any preliminary sketches. He did not worry about constructing his forms linearly but created shapes by means of color stains in a style that almost anticipated Impressionism.

Among Titian's colleagues in Venice were Lotto, Veronese, and Sebastian del Piombo, who collaborated with Titian in the completion of several works left unfinished by Giorgione. Most of these Venetian artists drew with charcoal, black chalk, or Italian stone, a material quite similar to our carbon pencil, though softer. The fact that these artists favored these materials rather than the metalpoint is understandable because Venetian painting emphasized color, which, when translated to drawing, implies a more thorough and expressive pencil stroke.

67

68

69

70

Fig. 66 (above). Titian, Tiziano Vecellio (1490-1576). *Portrait of a Young Woman.* Charcoal and white chalk on ochre-gray tinted paper. Uffizi Gallery, Florence.

Fig. 67. Sebastiano del Piombo (1485-1547). *Naked Woman Standing.* Charcoal and white chalk on blue-tinted paper. Louvre, Paris.

Fig. 68. Jacobo Tintoretto (1518-1594). *Study of the Roman Bust of Emperor Vitellius.* Black chalk and white chalk. Staatliche Museum, Munich.

Fig. 69. Paolo Veronese (1528-1588). *Head of a Woman.* Black chalk and white chalk on blue paper. Art Institute of Chicago.

Fig. 70. Lorenzo Lotto (1480-1556). *Head of a Bearded Man.* Black chalk and white chalk on dyed *verdaccio.* János Scholz, New York.

the renaissance in europe: dürer

Albrecht Dürer was an outstanding engraver and draftsman with a tremendous talent for assimilating new ideas. A German, Dürer traveled constantly, introducing Italian ways and ideas to Northern Europe, listening to everybody and watching everything, learning new things, and teaching what he knew. During his journeys to Italy he apprenticed with Bellini, Titian, Leonardo, and Mantegna. He lectured on the art of woodcut illustration, and thanks to his efforts, this art form spread all over Europe.

Dürer's work consists of many woodcuts, engravings, drawings, watercolors an unusual medium for that time, in which Dürer pioneered and oil paintings, as well as treatises on medicine, fortifications, and artistic theory.

Woodcuts & Etching

At the beginning of the sixteenth century, Albrecht Dürer was the supreme master of wood and copper engraving in Europe, Wood cutting (xylography) is done in a thick wooden block. On its even and polished surface the artist engraves an image with a chisel and a gouge, cutting away the parts meant to be white in the final picture, so that the parts meant to be in black stand out on the surface. After this, the surface is inked. A sheet of paper is placed against the block and rubbed with a burnisher.

Thus we get the first proof. An etching is engraved on a copper plate which has been coated with an acid-proof resin. The plate is engraved with a burin which removes the resin and leaves the metal exposed. Then the plate is soaked in nitric acid, which dissolves the metal in the exposed parts. After removing the rest of the resin, the plate is inked so that the ink fills the grooves. Finally, a proof is printed by pressing a sheet of paper against the plate with the help of a hand printing press.

71

72

Fig. 72. Jan van der Straet, known as Stradamus (1530-1605). Printing with Copper Plates in the Sixteenth Century. Etching from "Nova reperta et alia".

73

74

Fig. 71. Albrecht Dürer (1471-1528). *Christ on the Cross.* Lead metalpoint and white chalk on cream paper. Louvre, Paris.

Fig. 73 (right). Albrecht Dürer. *Girl Dresses as a Dutch Woman.* Sepia watercolor and white tempera (gouache). National Gallery of Art, Washington.

Fig. 74 (far right). Albrecht Dürer. *The Four Horsemen of the Apocalypse* (detail). Engraving in xylography.

the renaissance in europe

Culturally speaking, one of the most significant achievements of Italy was the artistic conquest of Europe. Except for a few exceptional artists, such as those in the workshop of the Flemish painter Pieter Brueghel, the influence of Italy was ever-present during the fifteenth and sixteenth centuries in the workshops of European artists. The new theories about perspective (Ucello and Piero), the rediscovery of anatomy by means of dissection drawings (Leonardo and Michelangelo), the latest techniques of *sfumato* and chiaroscuro (Leonardo), as well as the Renaissance subjects with man as the center, fascinated Dürer, inspired Holbein, suggested new subjects to Gossaert (also called Mabuse), and compelled most artists to travel to Italy in order to grasp the essence of the Renaissance.

Unfortunately for art, the Renaissance came to an end around the beginning of the sixteenth century, when the Protestant Reformation began. In 1527, the army of Charles V conquered and sacked Rome, causing the bankers to flee and the artists to disperse. Around that time artists abandoned the quiet classicism of Renaissance art in search of a more intellectual style that came to be known as Mannerism.

Fig. 75 (right). Hans Holbein, the Younger (1497-1543). *Portrait of Anna Meyer.* Colored chalks. Kunstmuseum, Basel.

Fig. 76 (below). Hans Baldung, also called Grien (1484-1545). *Saturn.* Charcoal. Albertina Museum, Vienna.

76

77

78

Fig. 78. Pieter Brueghel, the Elder (1525-1569). *The Painter and the Critic.* Bister ink. Albertina Museum, Vienna.

79

Fig. 79. Jan Gossaert, also called Mabuse (c. 1478-1532). *The Fall of Man.* Dark sepia ink. Albertina Museum, Vienna.

Fig. 77. Jean Clouet (1485/90-1541). *A Lady.* Charcoal and sanguine. British Museum, London.

the baroque period: the drawing academies

When Luther began the Protestant Reformation in Wittemberg, in 1517, the Roman Catholic Church answered with a bigoted attitude toward customs and art. After the Counter-Reformation, the church became more tolerant and tried to develop a more imposing look to reassert its authority. Icons were renewed. More emphasis was put on the representation of supernatural concepts such as the triumph of faith, the papacy, saints, the Immaculate Conception, heaven and glory. On the other hand, kings and princes were so keen on splendor that they promoted huge projects and sumptuous decorations. Thus arose the Baroque style: a visual, dynamic type of art characterized by extravagant forms and gesticulating figures. It is said that Correggio and his imitators and even Michelangelo in his *Last Judgment* had already begun the Baroque period. However, the ones who really determined the new style were the Carracci family and Caravaggio. The Carraccis were a Bolognese family of three artists: Ludovico, the eldest, the first artist to systematize the teaching of life drawing, and his cousins, Annibale and Agostino. The three of them founded an academy in Bologna. This academy became the School of Bologna, frequented by artists such as Domenichino, Reni, Albani... Drawing and classical painting were taught there following the great masters of the Renaissance, and avoiding the artificial realism of Mannerism. Annibale was the greatest of the Carraccis. He had many followers and painted, among other things, the ceiling of the Farnese Gallery, Rome, considered among the best frescoes of the sixteenth century. Academies of drawing proliferated throughout the sixteenth and seventeenth centuries not only in Italy but all over Europe.

80

82

Fig. 80. Annibale Carracci (1560-1609). *Portrait of a Member of the Mascheroni Family.* Sanguine and white chalk on sepia-tinted paper.

Fig. 81. Agostino Carracci (1557-1602). *Dead Man Lying Down.* Sanguine and white chalk. János Scholz, New York.

Fig. 82. Ludovico Carracci (1555-1619). *Head of a Woman Looking Up to the Left.* Charcoal and white chalk on beige paper. Metropolitan Museum of Art, New York.

the baroque period: caravaggio

When the Carraccis had already established the Baroque as a theatrical and sentimental, though careful and harmonious, style, the revolutionary style of Caravaggio appeared, Baroque as well. It was said that he had come to this world "to destroy the art of painting" (Poussin), though other artists like Rubens admired him and copied his paintings. Caravaggio was the founder of the naturalistic style, which was followed by all the great masters of the century: Ribera and Velázquez in Spain, La Tour and the Le Nain brothers in France, Rubens in Flanders, and Rembrandt in the Netherlands. Unfortunately, we do not know of any drawings by Caravaggio. However, we do know that he used to begin his paintings without sketching first, painting and drawing all at once, as Titian and Velázquez were known to do.

Fig. 83. Pietro da Cortona, Pietro Berrettini (1596-1669). *Study of a Young Woman.* Black chalk, sanguine, and white chalk on gray paper. Albertina Museum, Vienna.

84

Fig. 84. Pier Francesco Mola (1612-1666). *Figure Running with a Stone in the Hand.* Charcoal and Sanguine. British Museum, London.

Fig. 85. Le Guide (1575-1642). *Head of a Youth.* Black chalk and sanguine. Hermitage, Leningrad.

86

Fig. 86. Nicholas Poussin (1595-1665). *Landscape with River.* Ink and bister wash. Albertina Museum, Vienna.

85

87

Fig. 87. Peter Paul Rubens (1577-1640). *Young Woman with Crossed Hands* (detail). Black chalk, charcoal, sanguine, and white chalk on cream paper. Boimans-Van Beuningen Museum, Rotterdam. Ruben's biographers say that he drew with an extraordinary rapidity and a confident and expressive line. These qualities are evident in this drawing: The contours of the hair are spontaneous and the features are drawn "alla prima." Note the subtle gradations of the eyes, nose, and mouth, with just the right values and contours. Note also the range of color achieved using only black chalk, red sanguine, white chalk, and a cream-colored background.

rubens

In 1621, Peter Paul Rubens sent a letter to William Trumbull, a man closely connected with the English court, accepting the return of a picture painted for the English ambassador to Holland. In that letter Rubens also promised to paint another picture "entirely himself" and added, in answer to the ambassador's complaints, that he had never been told whether the picture was supposed to be Ruben's work alone or simply dictated to his apprentices.

Indeed, many of the pictures attributed to Rubens were painted by his followers and pupils. Rubens was a very busy man. In addition to his work as an artist, he was also a diplomat in the service of the governors of Flanders, and took on assignments given by kings and princes. To meet all these obligations and still be able to paint more than 2,500 paintings during his lifetime, Rubens organized his work and workshop employing followers and pupils such

as van Dyck, Jordaens, Snyders, van Unden, and Wildens. The whole team worked from drawings and watercolor sketches by Rubens. Sometimes Rubens did not participate in the final resolution of these paintings. Only when the patron demanded greater accuracy did Rubens take part in painting the head, hands, or arms of the most visible figures. No wonder then that Rubens's artistic capacity is judged nowadays both by his drawings and sketches and by the finished works. His biographers recount that he drew amazingly fast, with clear, long, and expressive lines. He preferred cream-colored paper and charcoal or black stone. To emphasize light and brightness, he used white chalk, or sanguine if the color of flesh was required.

Fig. 88 (below, left). Peter Paul Rubens. *The Fall of the Convicted Man.* Charcoal. British Museum, London.

Fig. 89 (below, right). Peter Paul Rubens. *Lion.* Black, yellow, and white chalk on gray-sienna paper. Louvre, Paris.

Fig. 90 (left). Peter Paul Rubens. *Male Figure Bending Down Seen from Behind.* Sienna and white chalk on beige paper.

88

89

90

Rembrandt is another example of a master painter and draftsman. In 1851, the painter Delacroix dared to foretell that one day Rembrandt's art would be regarded as superior to Raphael's. In response, Ingres called Delacroix a heretic. However, Delacroix's prophesy has been fulfilled. Today, Rembrandt is regarded as one of the great masters of the art of painting and drawing, as good as Raphael, if not better.

About 600 paintings are attributed to Rembrandt, along with 300 etchings combined with drypoint, and about 2,000 drawings, many of which are executed in sanguine and wash. In addition to Rubens, other contemporanies of Rembrandt were Jordaens, van Dyck, and Teniers in Flanders; Ribera, Zurbarán, Velázquez, and Murillo in Spain; and the Le Nain family, Poussin, La Tour, and Claude Lorrain in France.

93

91

94

Fig. 91 (left). Rembrandt van Rijn (1606-1669). *Biblical Scene*. Bister and watercolor wash. Albertina Museum, Vienna.

Fig. 92. Anton van Dyck (1599-1641). *Pentecost*. Sienna ink. Hermitage, Leningrad.

Fig. 93. Rembrandt (1606-1669). *The Omval at the River Amstel*. Etching. British Museum, London.

Fig. 94. Rembrandt. *Self-portrait Expressing Terror*. Rijksmuseum, Amsterdam.

Fig. 95. Rembrandt. *Cleopatra*. Sanguine on cream paper. Villiers David, London.

95

the eighteenth century in italy and england

In the eighteenth century, many Italian artists, such as Ricci, Canaletto, Guardi, Piranesi, Carlevari, and Panini, used to draw *vedutas* (views of Venice and the ruins of ancient Rome), which were reproduced as etchings printed in sepia and black. These *vedutas* were to be sold to foreign visitors, particularly English tourists who wanted a souvenir of their visit to ancient Rome. While looking at those sheets printed in black, someone had the idea of coloring them with transparent watercolors. Paul Sandby, "the father of watercolor," according to the English, developed this work into a fine art. By the end of the eighteenth century, artists such as Cozens, Pars, Towne, Gritin, and Turner made watercolor the English national art. In Italy, Giovanni Battista Tiepolo known for his wall paintings and frescoes, left hundreds of wash drawings as sketches for his decorative art.

Fig. 96. Canaletto, Giovanni Antonio Canal (1697-1768). *Country House and Tower on the Edge of the Small Lake.* Sienna and ochre wash and ink. Hermitage, Leningrad.

96

97

Fig. 97. Francesco Guardi (1712-1793). *Houses on the Grand Canal of Venice.* Sienna wash and ink. Albertina Museum, Vienna.

Fig. 98. Giambattista Tiepolo (1696-1770). *St. Jerome in the Desert Hearing Angels.* Sienna wash and ink. National Gallery of Art, Washington.

Fig. 99. Giambattista Piranesi (1720-1778). *Prisons.* Engraving. Beid Colnaghi, London.

99

france: the rococo period

During the Renaissance, Italy was the artistic center of the world, and during the Baroque period Flanders had that distinction. After that, France determined styles and tendencies in art. The new French style was called Rococo. It inherited from the Baroque its luxury, sensuousness, and ornamentation. This new style changed elegant ornamentation into fine arrangements and substituted a more intimate and delicate representation for the expressive force and dynamism of the Baroque style.

Fig. 100. Jean-Antoine Watteau (1684-1721). *Three Studies of the Head of a Black Youth*. Charcoal, sanguine, and white chalk on cream paper. Louvre, Paris.

Famous artists of the Rococo period were Watteau, Boucher, and Fragonard. Watteau was regarded as a painter of *fêtes galantes*. He was an admirer and a follower of Rubens. A great draftsman, Watteau kept thick sketchbooks filled with hundreds of drawings of figures, heads, hands, and clothes, which he used for his paintings. Boucher was a pupil of Watteau and excelled as a decorator, a draftsman, and a painter of charmingly irreverent intimate and mythological scenes.

101

Fig. 101. Jean-Honoré Fragonard (1732-1806). *Angelica Appears Before Sacripante*. Charcoal with touches of ochre, gray, and sienna watercolors. Museum of Art. Princeton University.

Fig. 102. François Boucher (1703-1770). *Diana Sleeping*. Sienna chalk and white chalk on beige paper. School of Fine Arts. Paris.

102

the eighteenth century in england and spain

Fig. 103. Francisco de Goya y Lucientes (1746-1828). *The Disasters of War: With or Without Reason.* Etching. National Chalcography, Madrid. Goya is an exceptional Spanish artist. In addition to his well-known paintings, he made hundreds of drawings and engravings on social subjects and as protests against war. These drawings are admired the world over for their drawing quality and powerful imagery.

Fig. 104. Thomas Gainsborough (1727-1788). *Study of a Woman*, Possibly for the Painting of the Stream of Richmond. Charcoal and sienna chalk with white gouache on buff paper. British Museum, London.

104

Fig. 105. Alexander Cozens (c. 1717-1786). *Composition for a Landscape.* India ink. British Museum, London.

Fig. 107 (right). Pierre Paul Proud'hon (1758-1823). *Venus.* Charcoal and white chalk on blue paper. National Gallery of Art, Washington.

Fig. 106. Jean Auguste Dominique Ingres (1780-1867). Study for the Painting *Turkish Bath.* Lead pencil. Louvre, Paris.

Fig. 108 (far right). Jean-Baptiste Camille Corot (1796-1875). *Landscape.* Charcoal. British Museum, London.

neoclassicism

On July 14, 1789, the Bastille was stormed and the French Revolution erupted. Jacques-Louis David, the painter of the Revolution, established the grounds for a new classical style, a reflection of the ancient Roman republic. This new style was called Neoclassicism. Its outstanding representative is Jean-August Dominique Ingres, a proponent of classicism and an exceptional draftsmen. Ingres is known for his sketches and portraits in lead pencil, as well as his paintings. He was also known for his teachings, such as, "you paint the same as you draw," "the details are tell-tales one has to keep under control," or "the good draftsman must keep an eye on everything." During his lifetime, Ingres was a controversial painter because of his academic style. His dogmatism and sensitivity to criticism often led to a conflict with critics. His most passionate enemies were Géricault and Delacroix.

The German Anton Mengs was also a prominent artist of that period: He was one of the best-known artists of the Neoclassical period, a child prodigy who could make great pastel portraits at thirteen and who was appointed chief painter of the Dresden court at seventeen. In France, Proud'hon, who already hinted at Romanticism, and Corot, who began as a classicist and whose last pictures placed him close to Impressionism, were also important.

106

107

108

romanticism and realism

Romanticism is a passionate reflection of the imaginative and individualistic spirit of the nineteenth century. Realism, on the other hand, rejects the great historical subjects and the dramatic contents of Romanticism to develop a style whose intention is to reproduce nature faithfully. Delacroix was an important spokesman of Romanticism. A great colorist, he was a master of sketches and drawings. Géricault in France, and Fuseli and Blake in England were other prominent romantic painters. Daumier, Rousseau, Courbet, and Millet in France, and Fortuny in Spain were the fore-

Fig. 109. Eugène Delacroix (1798-1863). *Study of a Female Nude for the Death of Sardanapalus. Pastel. Louvre, Paris.*

Fig. 110. Gustave Courbet (1819-1877). *Self-Portrait, Man with Pipe.* Charcoal. Wadsworth Atheneum, Hartford, Conn.

most Realist artists of this period. Turner, Corot, Boudin, and the American Homer began as Romantics and went on to pioneer Impressionism. It is notable that all the artists of this period were excellent draftsmen, particularly Delacroix, with his thick sketchbook filled with hundreds of drawings; Blake, who was an illustrator of books and of his own poetry; Daumier, painter of social themes; Fortuny, a great watercolorist; Corot, with his studies of nature; and Homer, an illustrator and watercolorist.

Impressionism

Monet, Manet, Pissarro, Renoir, Degas, Sisley, Cezanne, Boudin, Morisot . . . In the nineteenth century, during the sixties and seventies, the great jury of the Salon de Paris refused the pictures of these artists. In trying to find outlets for their works, they organized the so-called Salon des Refusés (the Exhibition of the Rejected). The exhibition was a complete failure. In the *Figaro* newspaper an account of the exhibition read: "five or six lunatics —one of them a woman— a group of poor devils tempted by a foolish ambition, have joined together to exhibit their pictures . . . a terrible spectacle of human vanity bordering on madness." The title of one of the pictures exhibited was *Impression, Soleil Levant (Impres-*

109

impressionism

sion, Sunrise) by Monet, which inspired the critic M. Leroi to ridicule the members of the group by calling them Impressionists. The word *Impressionism* was included by these artists in their first group exhibition in 1874.

Impressionism meant a real revolution: It entailed a radical change in the colors of the artist's palette, in composition, in subject matter, and in technique. It also changed the environment of the painter from the academic studio to the outdoors.

All Impressionists relied on drawing: Degas, with his extraordinary pastels, is perhaps the master draftsman of all time; Toulouse Lautrec is known for his sketches in colored pencils or chalk; and Van Gogh showed the same expressiveness in his pencil and ink drawings that he did in his paintings. The drawings of Impressionists are fine examples of a style that became a prelude to modern art.

Figs. 111, 112. Edouard Manet (1823-1883). *Portrait of Madame Jules Guillemet.* Charcoal. Hermitage, Leningrad. This drawing served as a preliminary sketch for the finished painting shown in Fig. 111, (above right).

111

112

113

114

115

Fig. 113. Georges Seurat (1859-1891). *Woman Embroidering.* Conté crayon. Metropolitan Museum of Art, New York.

Fig. 114. Edgar Degas (1834-1917). *After the Bath.* Pastel. Durand Ruel Collection, Paris.

Fig. 115. Vincent van Gogh (1853-1890). *La Grau Seen from Montmajour.* Pencil, red pen, pen, brown and black ink on Whatman paper. Rijksmuseum, Amsterdam.

drawings of modern masters

It is impossible to summarize in a few lines the vast number of drawings, noted artists, and styles of art that exist in the twentieth century. But the following comprise the major artistic movements that have developed in this century: Post-impressionism, the foremost artists of which are Van Gogh, Gaugin, and Cézanne; Pointillism, in which Seurat is the major figure; Fauvism, including Matisse, whose artists were labeled *fauves* (wild Beasts), because of their shocking synthesis of strong colors; the Nabis movement, headed by Bonnard and Vuillard, who later drifted toward Intimism, a style of art that focuses on intimate domestic interiors; Cubism, headed by Picasso and Braque and followed by Juan Gris (however, Picasso goes beyond the scope of Cubism. He was one of the greatest draftsmen in the history of art, and his work covers a multitude of styles); Symbolism, led by the German Max Ernst; Surrealism, whose main representative, Salvador Dalí, has expressed himself through drawing as well as through painting; Expressionism, represented by Nolde, Ensor, Modigliani, and Grosz, for whom drawing is of major importance; Metaphysical painting and drawing, with De Chirico and Carra; Futurism, which exalted machines, speed, and, in some

Fig. 120. Pablo Picasso (1881-1973). *The Beggar.* Watercolor on ochre paper. Picasso Museum, Barcelona.

116

118

117

119

Fig. 116. John Singer Sargent (1856-925). Lead pencil. Fogg Art Museum, Harvard University, Cambridge.

Fig. 117. Ramón Casas (1866-1932). *Portrait of Joaquín Alvarez Quintero.* Charcoal. Museum of Modern Art, Barcelona.

Fig. 118. Emil Nolde (1867-1956). *Portrait of an Italian.* Xylograph. Albertina Museum, Vienna.

Fig. 119. Edward Hopper (1882-1967). *Self-Portrait.* Charcoal. National Portrait Gallery, Washington, D.C.

cases, the violence of twentieth-century life; Abstract art, which began with a watercolor by Kandinsky and was developed by Mondrian; Op(tical) art, of which Vasarely is a major figure; and Pop(ular) art, among whose major followers is the American artist R. B. Kitaj, an exceptional draftsman of figurative art.

121

123

Fig. 121. Henri Matisse (1869-1954). *Woman in an Armchair.* Charcoal.

122

Fig. 122. Aubrey Beardsley (1872-1898). *The Wagnerians.* India ink. Victoria and Albert Museum, London.

Fig. 123. Fernand Léger (1881-1955). *Face and Hands.* Ink over pencil. Museum of Modern Art, New York.

drawings of modern masters

124

125

Fig. 124. Georg Grosz (1893-1959). *Men in a Café*. Lead pencil. British Museum, London.

Fig. 125. Walter Sickert (1860-1942). *Woman in Front of a Mirror*. Blue pencil and white pencil on gray pencil.

Fig. 126. R. B. Kitaj (1932-). *Marynka Smoking*. Pastel over charcoal pencil. Collection of the artist.

Fig. 127. Egon Schiele (1890-1918). *The Artist and His Model*. Lead pencil. Albertina Museum, Vienna.

126

127

materials, tools, and techniques

One day a few hairs came out of my brush and got stuck on the picture. I then painted a bird's nest.

how, where, and with what to draw

The essentials needed for drawing are: a 2B pencil, paper, an eraser, and some sort of drawing board. Of course, the pencil can be softer or harder, the paper can be high or low quality, white or colored. Or, instead of a pencil, you can use another drawing instrument, such as charcoal, crayon, chalk, colored pencils, pen, or even a brush for drawing with watercolor, or ink. However, this variety of media does not alter the basic idea that to produce the best drawing of all you need only paper and pencil. Drawing is the basic graphic technique. It is the perfect means for obtaining fine-art drawings, such as figure studies, portraits, sketches, composition studies, and preliminary drawings for finished pieces; or for commercial art, such as illustrations, television commercials, and advertisements. But, how does one go about learning to draw? Where? With what? Let's go step by step, beginning with the "how and where" first. We'll explore places where you can draw, in a studio or outdoors, and the basic equipment you'll need: furniture, lighting, sketchbooks, drawing boards, easels, and materials. After this, we'll look inside the studio at drawing techniques. We'll begin by looking at the illustrations on these pages.

Fig. 130 (below). Sitting on a stool, a chair, or an armchair leaning the board against your lap or a table, or, as in this picture, against the back of a chair are good positions for drawing whether you are working in your own studio or in a classroom with a model. These positions for drawing come in handy when there is no easel available or when you are drawing on the site.

Fig. 131 (right). When you draw outdoors, you can use a cardboard portfolio, or clipboard, as a support, resting it on a stone, a ledge, or any other convenient surface, while you use anything suitable as a seat. This way you will only need to carry a pencil, an eraser, and the portfolio. But don't forget to bring a pair of metal clips, always essential to keep the paper smooth.

128

Fig. 128. As shown in this illustration, it's perfectly possible to draw while standing, by holding the portfolio or the board with one hand and drawing with the other. This is a satisfactory position when doing quick sketches or a drawing that can be completed in a short time.

129

Fig. 129 (above). When you are working outside the studio and must transport your drawing materials (such as pencils, charcoals, sketchbooks, erasers, stumps) to a site, it's ideal to use a box similar to the one reproduced here. These one is more commonly used for oil paints, but it makes a perfect container for drawing materials. It's small, just 12 1/2 x 7 in. (32 x 20 cm) and very portable.

130

132

131

Fig. 132. It's convenient to keep several portfolios of different sizes in the studio in order to store your paper, to keep your finished drawings, or to use as a support when drawing outdoors. Note the black portfolio with the metal handle to help in transporting the drawings or your paper supply.

Fig. 134 (below). This is a workshop easel complete with wheels set up for drawing, with a wooden board and drawing paper held by two clips. This classic model allows the artist to tilt the working surface forward in order to work more comfortably and to eliminate reflections. The distance between the seat and the easel enables the artist to come in closer when drawing in detail, or to lean back when observing the whole.

Fig. 133 (below). This is the short-legged version of the folding easel-box. Although this box is often used for oil painting, it works just as well for drawing when you work with a portfolio or a wooden board as a support and drawing paper instead of a canvas. The box can be used as well, not only for oil paints, but for drawing materials and tools. To complete your equipment, add a folding stool.

133

134

the studio: lighting and furnishing

135

A studio can be any room or any corner of a room in your home. It can be any spot where a table can be placed near a window. As for furniture, you'll need a simple board and a chair. Of course, there are much more elaborate types of studios such as studios set up specially for drawing.

In practice, when you are ready, the studio becomes a place where you may want to draw someone's portrait, sketch your cat, or make a figure study (particularly if you have hired a live model). The studio is also the place where you'll be alone to experience the emotion of drawing.

A 13 ft. × 10 ft. (4 m × 3 m) room, or larger, similar to the one shown in Fig. 135, with

138

Fig. 135. Here we have a painter's studio 3.5 m (11'6'') wide by 4.5 m (14'8'') long, drawn to scale, as are the dimensions of the furniture. Included is everything needed to work comfortably. Notice the direction of daylight from the left-hand side in relation to the table and the easel.

136

Fig. 136. This "scissor-style" drafting table, classic for drawing, has been available for over a hundred years. Its folding tabletop can be adjusted to the angle you wish.

Fig. 137. The modern table, like this "pioneer" by the U.S. manufacturer American, is both elegant and functional. It has a top that can be tilted at any angle, drawers for extra materials, and a crossbar to rest your feet on.

137

Fig. 138. This piece of furniture serves as a bookshelf or as counter with specially added drawers for storing paper and drawings. One of the drawers can be fitted with translucent glass with a lamp inside to use as a tracing table or for looking at slides.

similar furnishings, would make an ideal studio. The following is a list of the lighting and furnishings necessary for the professional studio.

Lighting
1. A window that lets in daylight
2. Table lamps
3. Auxiliary lamps
4. Lamp with extendable arm attached to the easel
5. Ceiling lights

Furnishings

A. Workshop easel
B. Drawing table with sloping board (Fig. 136)
C. Armchair
D. Auxiliary table
E-F-G. Glass table (Figs. 135, 138)
H. Several chairs or a sofa for the model
I. Three-legged stool for drawing at the easel

Take a look at the table shown on this page. It is designed for drawing with a tabletop easel that can take the form of a desk. The right-hand side is meant for keeping materials and tools within reach. The armchair is for drawing at the table, and the wheeled stool is for sitting at the easel.

Fig. 139. Here is a drawing of an artist drawing a portrait in his studio. Note the design of the table that has been especially made for the studio: The central board is adjustable and can be tilted to the desired angle; the auxiliary spaces on both sides are excellent storage areas, with drawers to keep the art materials and store the sketches and studies in progress. Note also the adjustable easel on top of the central board, the lamp with an articulated arm to direct the light, and the chair with attached wheels to allow for easy movement.

139

the studio: lighting and furnishing

Fig. 140. The materials and tools for drawing are many and varied: soft and hard lead pencils, charcoals, pastels, Conté crayons, pens and India ink. In addition, there are auxiliary materials that are also necessary. Note these in the photograph below:

1. Fixative spray to fix drawings done in pencil, charcoal, Conté crayon, or pastel. Fixative is not advisable for pastel drawings because it can alter the color.

2. Graduated metal ruler, 50 or 70 cm (12 or 15 in.) long. A ruler should be made of metal so that it won't be damaged when cutting paper or cardboard with an X-Acto knife or razor blade.

3. A metric triangular scale rule 30 cm (1 ft.) long.

4. Set square and triangle made of transparent plastic.

5. Clip for securing paper to the board; the best clips are the widest ones, the "bulldog" kind, which can be used not only to hold the paper but to stretch it when painting with watercolor.

6. Roll of adhesive tape, used to frame a wash or a watercolor before starting to paint. The tape is positioned like a frame and comes off easily when finished, leaving the edges perfectly clean and sharp.

7. Rubber cement used for gluing paper to paper, cardboard, or wood.

8. Paper towels, essential for painting washes, cleaning brushes, and erasing preliminary charcoal sketches.

9. Glass container for watercolor washes. When you use India ink, the water should be distilled. When painting outdoors, an unbreakable plastic container is advisable.

10. Pencil sharpener.

11. Sharpener made especially for lead pencils.

12. Pushpins to hold the paper to the board.

13. Razor blade or X-Acto knife to cut paper or cardboard.

14. Large scissors for cutting paper.

141

Fig. 141. A stand for large portfolios, for holding drawing papers, and for protecting works-in-progress and finished works, is essential in a studio.

140

drawing papers

With the exception of some specialized papers such as metallic paper, synthetic paper, or certain very thin silk paper, all forms of paper can be used for drawing. One of the most famous pastel drawings, *Vase with Flowers*, by the Post-Impressionist Odilon Redon, was drawn on cardboard.

The most available type of paper is medium-quality and smooth made of wood pulp and manufactured by machine or molds. High-quality papers such as Canson, Fabriano, Schoeller, Whatman, and Grumbacher contain a high percentage of rag and are made with great care. They are also expensive, which is why some manufacturers don't make them. High-quality papers can be distinguished by a mark bearing the name of the manufacturer, which appears on the paper either stamped in relief or in the traditional watermark, which can be seen by holding the paper up to light. Among drawing papers commercially available, you can find the following textures:

A. Smooth paper
B. Fine-grain paper
C. Medium-grain paper, semi-rough
D. Coarse-grain paper, rough
E. Ingres paper, white and colored
F. Colored papers
G. Canson colored paper (called Mi-Teintes)

There are other more unusual kinds of paper such as rice paper, particularly suitable for sumi-e; couché "grattage" paper, suitable for drawings that are meant to imitate woodcuts, parole papers lined with cloth or laminated with an aluminum sheet, and polyester paper.

A. *Smooth paper* has an almost imperceptible grain. It is pressed smooth while hot, and is often called hot-pressed paper. Particularly suitable for pen and pencil drawing, smooth paper provides an excellent surface for developing contrasts and light and shade effects. It is very suitable for drawing portraits.

B. *Fine-grain paper* is very good for drawing with graphite pencil, wax, or colored pencils. The grain of the paper enhances the final result without losing the harmony and the smoothness of shading and tonal gradations.

C. *Medium-grain paper* is particularly suitable for drawing with pastels, crayon, colored chalks, wash, and for watercolor painting.

D. *Coarse-grain paper* is generally used for watercolor painting.

E. *Ingres paper* has been on the market for more than one hundred years. It is excellent for charcoal drawing. Its special woven texture is clearly visible against the light, and evident when the drawing is finished. Ingres is also a good surface for oil crayons and pastels. Today, however, there is a tendency to use medium-grain or coarse-grain papers when drawing with colored media.

F. *Canson colored paper (Mi-Teintes)* is a fine-grain paper without ridges. It is manufactured in a wide range of colors (see page 57, Fig. 146). The grain on the "right" side is coarser than on the back, although the quality is the same on both sides, with the advantage that the artist can choose between a coarser and a finer side. Mi-Teintes provides a good texture and an ideal sizing for drawing with charcoal, chalk, crayon, pastels, and colored pencils.

Fig. 142. To distinguish the best-quality drawing paper, manufacturers stamp their dry mark in one corner of the sheet, or they print their logo with the traditional watermark, which can be seen by holding the paper up to the light.

142

drawing papers

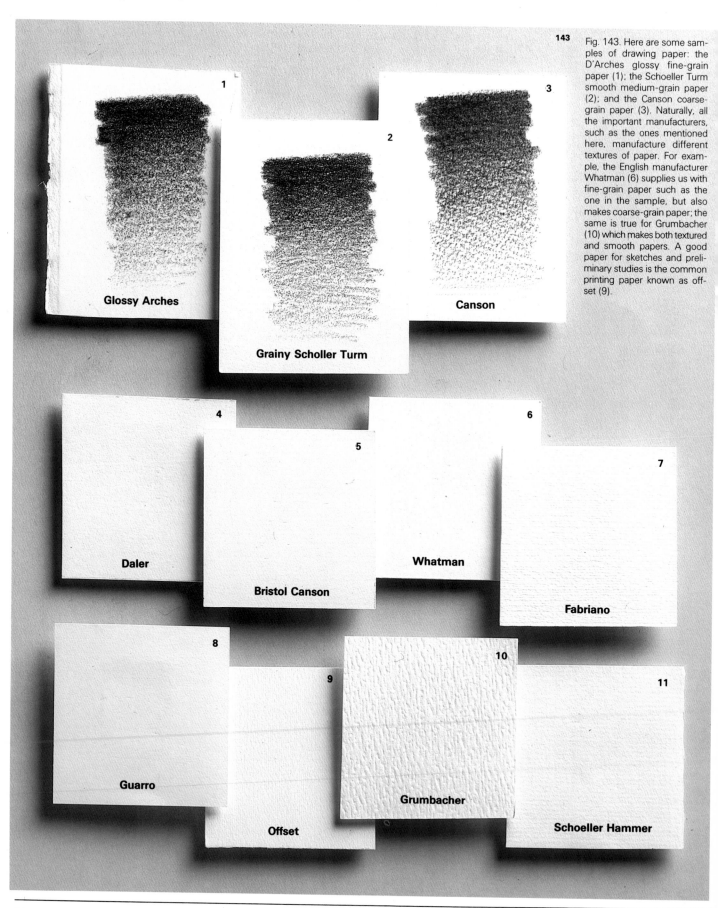

143

Fig. 143. Here are some samples of drawing paper: the D'Arches glossy fine-grain paper (1); the Schoeller Turm smooth medium-grain paper (2); and the Canson coarse-grain paper (3). Naturally, all the important manufacturers, such as the ones mentioned here, manufacture different textures of paper. For example, the English manufacturer Whatman (6) supplies us with fine-grain paper such as the one in the sample, but also makes coarse-grain paper; the same is true for Grumbacher (10) which makes both textured and smooth papers. A good paper for sketches and preliminary studies is the common printing paper known as offset (9).

Glossy Arches

Grainy Scholler Turm

Canson

Daler

Bristol Canson

Whatman

Fabriano

Guarro

Offset

Grumbacher

Schoeller Hammer

Figs. 144 and 145. This is a collection of colored paper samples, made by Canson, called Mi-Teintes. Most paper manufacturers, such as Fabriano from Italy, De Wint from England, Guarro from Spain, and Canson from France make medium- or rough-grain colored papers for drawing. Colored papers are especially recommended for charcoal, Conté crayon, pastels, colored pencils, and highlighting with white chalk.

Fig. 146. Francesc Serra. Charcoal and Cronté crayon on colored paper (detail). Private collection.

144

145

146

papers: sizes and weights

Paper is counted in *reams* and *quires*. A *ream* is 500 sheets; a *quire* 25, regardless of size. The weight of the ream and its conversion to pounds per square foot determine how thick the paper actually is. Paper can range in weight from a medium weight to the heavy and superheavy. Drawing paper is sold in single sheets or mounted on cardboard with the following standard measurements: 4 × 6 in., 5 × 7 in., 8 × 10 in., 9 × 12 in., 11 × 14 in., 14 × 17 in., 18 × 24 in., 15 × 20 in., 15 × 22 in., 19 × 24 in., 24 × 36 in. (10 × 15 cm, 12 × 18 cm, 20 × 25 cm, 23 × 30 cm, 28 × 36 cm, 36 × 43 cm, 46 × 61 cm, 38 × 50 cm, 38 × 56 cm, 48 × 61 cm, 61 × 92 cm).

It can also be found in rolls of 36, 42, and 60 in. (92, 102, 152 cm) wide × 10 yds (920 cm) long, in blocks of 20 or 25 sheets bound by the spiral system, or glued together on all four edges and backed by thick cardboard, thus forming a compact unit that keeps its shape. This block system is ideal for wash and watercolor papers. Keep in mind that most papers for wash and watercolor painting are perfectly suitable for pencil drawing, charcoal, crayon, chalk, and pastels. There are some exceptions, however. One is the coarse-grain paper specially manufactured for watercolor painting. Another exception is the grainless paper that is particularly suitable for drawing with pen.

Of course, sizes differ from country to country. For example, Great Britain has six different sizes, from the smallest 1/2 Imperial, 381 × 559 mm (15 × 22 in.) —to the largest— Antiquarian, 787 × 1346 mm (31 × 52 in.).

147

148

Fig. 147. Drawing paper is sold in individual sheets, in pads glued to cardboard, and in rolls (maximum size: 2 m 6 ft wide x 10 m 30 ft long). As shown in the illustration, some papers have irregular edges called barbs; this is characteristic of handmade paper.

Fig. 148. Drawing paper is also sold in spiral-bound pads, and in sketchbooks where the paper edges have been glued together.

MAKES OF GOOD QUALITY DRAWING PAPER

Arches	France
Canson & Montgolfier	France
Daler	England
Fabriano	Italy
Grumbacher	U.S.A.
Guarro	Spain
Schoeller Parole	Germany
Whatman	England

attaching, mounting and stretching paper

While you are drawing, paper must rest on a drawing board or be attached to one. The drawing board provides a smooth, even surface. The paper should be attached to the board with tape, or, better yet, with metal clips like those shown in Fig. 140.

However, when it comes to working with a medium such as watercolor, which requires moistening the paper, special methods must be used because the paper can become warped from the wetness. Obviously a warped watercolor, marred by an uneven, wrinkled surface, cannot be regarded as professional. To solve this problem, look at Figs. 150–155, where you can see how to mount and stretch paper with gummed tape. Securing your paper to the board can also be done with drawing pins. To achieve a taut surface, you can attach several clips around the paper or attach the paper with metal staples using a staple gun such as the type used by carpenters (see Fig. 153). Stapling can be done only when the paper is thick enough, 200 to 225 grams (20 to 25 lbs.) at least. If the paper is thinner than that, you'll need to mount it.

149

150

151

152

Fig. 149. When you're painting in washes with India ink or watercolor and your paper is not thick enough, you'll need to moisten, mount, and stretch the paper in order to prevent it from warping. To saturate the paper sufficiently, hold it in both hands and wet it under the tap or submerge it in water for at least two minutes.

Fig. 150. After wetting the paper, lay it on a wooden board, and smooth it out so that there are no bulges or wrinkles.

Fig. 151. Secure one side of the paper with a strip of gummed tape.

Fig. 152. Continue to tape the other sides until the paper is framed. Then, let it dry horizontally for four to five hours. You will then be able to paint on a smooth, taut surface, without any danger of its buckling.

Figs. 153 and 154. A paper that has been moistened can be also stretched by fastening it with metal staples from a staple gun. If the paper is heavy enough (more than 200 gr-20 lb.), the stretching can be done by using clips.

153

154

155

Fig. 155. When drawing in charcoal, Conté crayon, colored pencil, or pastel, it's not necessary to mount or stretch the paper. You only need to secure the paper to a board with pushpins or metal clips.

the lead pencil

The graphite pencil, more commonly known as the lead pencil, is the most frequently used tool for drawing. Graphite is a solid mineral that has a metallic brightness and a waxy, greasy consistency. It was discovered in Cumberland, England, in 1560, but it was not until 1640 that it reached France as an implement of drawing. In 1792, during the French Revolution, England broke its ties with France and stopped supplying France with graphite. It was then that the French engineer and chemist Nicolas Jacques Conté developed the Conté crayon, composed of a mixture of graphite and clay and covered with cedarwood. Conté also developed soft lead and hard lead pencils to create darker or lighter effects by changing the amount of graphite in relation to the clay.

The original quality of these early pencils has been improved. Today, manufacturers make pencils of different quality and gradations, namely:

1. *High-quality pencils with seventeen gradations* (Fig. 157). Those marked with a *B* (soft), will give you a darker line and are meant for general drawing. Those marked with an *H* (hard) give a lighter line and are often used for drafting or mechanical drawing. *HB* and *F* are intermediate grades and are good for general work.

Fig. 156. Varieties of graphite pencil from right to left: three pencils of a superior quality 6B, 2B, HB (A, B, C); school quality pencil n°. 2, equivalent to the superior quality pencil B (D); all-graphite pencil that consists entirely of graphite lead, and supplied in different grades (E); graphite lead with a 5.6 mm diameter made by Koh-i-noor (F); Koh-i-noor graphite sticks, supplied in different grades (G, H); Staedtler Mars automatic pencil with a diameter capacity for leads ranging from 9H to 4B (I); Caran D'Ache automatic pencil with a special diameter for soft-graded leads, from 4B to 8B (J); Faber-Castell carpenter pencil of a medium grade (K); Stabilotone pencil with a soft lead 1 cm(1/3-in.) diameter (L).

9H	8H	7H	6H	5H	4H	3H	2H	H	F	HB	B	2B	3B	4B	5B	6B	7B	8B

erasers

*2. School quality pencils with three gradations.
Soft*: Nº. 1, equivalent to 2B, and Nº. 2, equivalent to B. *Hard*: Nº. 3, equivalent to H.
The following is a list of pencils you'll need to begin drawing:

One 2B pencil: This is the most commonly used pencil. It's a soft pencil that not only gives intense blacks and soft grays but is also capable of producing thin lines.

One 4B and one 6B pencil: These are good for broad contours, quick sketches, and for blackening in dark areas.

One Nº. 2 school-quality pencil: For general use and light shading.

Pencils can also be found in different sizes and in different types, allowing for different strokes and effects. Note the *all-lead pencil*, the *5mm lead* used with clutch-type pencils, and the *graphite stick* (Fig. 156). The clutch-type pencils are specially devised to hold thick, soft leads such as a 6B.

Finally, note in Figs. 158 and 159, the function and possibilities of an eraser as a drawing tool.

Fig. 158. Kneaded erasers (A), or those made of plastic or rubber, which are more compact but just as smooth (B, D), are best for a waxy medium such as graphite, but they are not absorbent enough for erasing charcoal or pastel. For less waxy mediums, use erasers that are more pliable (C) and more absorbent. It is my opinion that erasers should be used only as a last resort; it is often better to start again than to damage and hurt the fiber of the paper.

Fig. 159. Erasers can be used as a means of drawing, to "open up" white areas and highlight edges. Look at these drawings of a half mask of Beethoven. On the left is the drawing before intensifying the shadows and picking out the lights (A). On the right the drawing was finished with the lights pulled out with an eraser (B).

Fig. 157. Graphite leads range from the soft B grades, to the medium grade HB, to the hard H grade. Note the intensity of the blacks in the B grade leads: the very softest and blackest is the 6B and the very hardest is the 9H. Artists generally prefer the softer leads (the 2B is the most commonly used pencil), but for filling in light tonal values and subtle details, it's often better to use the harder, more delicate H leads.

stumps

Fig. 160. Stumps come in different sizes. Use each stump for one color only, and keep one end for dark tones and the other for lighter tones.

The stump is a two-ended drawing tool. It is usually made of rolled paper, although some are made of felt or chamois leather. It is used for rubbing and blending, when you want to blend lines or areas drawn with lead pencil, charcoal, crayon, chalks, or pastels. You should use two or three stumps, thick, medium, or thin, and you should keep one of the ends for intense rubbing and the other for lighter rubbing.

For drawings that require the rubbing out of very small areas, use stumps as sharp as pencils. Some manufacturers make this kind of stump, like the one in Fig. 160 (far left). In Fig. 161 you can see the process for making your own stump by using a triangle of paper (see measurements in A); rolling it as if it were a hand-rolled cigarette (B – E) and closing it with a strip of gummed tape (F).

Fig. 161. Here is a way to build yourself a small stump with a sharp point for drawing small forms. Start with a triangle of spongy-type paper, such as newspaper. Then, roll this paper as if you were rolling a cigarette and secure the rolled paper with adhesive tape.

fingertip blending

Many artists prefer to draw and blend with their fingers rather than with paper stumps. There are several reasons for this: Fingertips are pliant; they easily adapt to the corrugations of the paper. Fingertips are moist; they combine this moisture, no matter how slight, with the waxy quality of graphite to produce a more intense black. Fingertips generate heat, and when they are rubbed against the graphite, the heat helps to blend and intensify the toned areas. Finally, fingers are simply a more convenient method of blending. Fig. 162 shows you how to blend using all five fingers, including the thumb. Notice that the little finger is used on its side which allows the tip to provide more accurate blending. Even the lower palm area can be employed in blending, as shown in Fig. 164.

163

A

Fig. 162. The tips of the fingers are an excellent way to blend areas created by lead pencils, charcoal, and pastels. Note in illustrations 3, 5, and 6, that the blended areas have been made with the tips of the fingers.

Fig. 163. Note in these examples that the grays obtained with a stump (B) are more intense than one in which a stump was not used (A).

B

162

1

2

3

4

5

6

164

Fig. 164. Different parts of the hand can be used for blending: the tips of the fingers, and occasionally, for large areas, the lower part of the palm.

how to hold the drawing instruments

You can draw standing in front of an easel, with the board in a vertical position; or you can draw sitting, with the board more or less slanted. In either case, you always draw in a position where you are likely to get the most complete view. When you are drawing, your distance from the paper should never be the same as if you were writing or doing fine detail work. In drawing, you need to be farther back.

The minimum distance from the artist's eyes to the drawing paper should be between 18 and 25 in. (45 and 65 cm).

In Fig. 165, you can see how the drawing position (absolutely standard, by the way) conditions our way of holding a pencil, stump, Conté crayon, or any other drawing tool. These are two ways of holding the pencil when you are doing relatively large drawings, say about 16 × 12 in. (40 × 30 cm). For very small drawings you would use the pencil similar to the way you would use it to write.

Fig. 166. *Standard position:* In this position the pencil is held slightly upward to facilitate the movement of the hand and the pencil. Keep in mind that when writing, you move your hand every five or six letters. When drawing, you hold the pencil in such a way that lines can be changed whenever and wherever you need. This allows for continuous lines without raising the pencil or stopping the hand.

Fig. 167. With the pencil inside the hand: This is the usual and most practical way for the artist to draw lines for shading and tonal gradations. The arm is stretched and follows the whole drawing, moving upward or downward, to the left or to the right without impediment.

Fig. 168. A variant of the pencil inside the hand: This way of holding the pencil allows you to press on the paper while drawing, to enhance a shaded area.

165

166

167

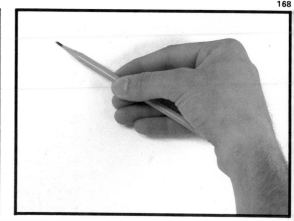
168

basic strokes with lead pencil

169

170

171

172

173

174

175

176

Here are some basic examples of tonal values made with lead pencils of different grades on smooth, fine-grain drawing paper.

Fig. 169. Note the difference of intensity and variety between the gradation made with soft 6D and 2B pencils (above), and the gradation made only with a hard H pencil (below).

Fig. 170. Diagonal strokes are the easiest and perhaps the most commonly used in drawing. This patch was made with a soft 2B pencil.

Fig. 171. A series of vertical lines made with a 2B pencil.

Fig. 172. The 2B pencil gives you a wide range of values. Notice how the direction of the lines develops and models the form.

Fig. 173. A medium-soft pencil, such as the school quality n°. 2, requires more pressure on the paper than does the 2B. That is why the texture of the paper is less evident here. By comparison, notice the intensity of the 2B pencil in the graduated strokes on the left.

Fig. 174. This tonal area was created by small circular strokes of a superior quality 2B pencil and a n°. 2 pencil. Note that the n°. 2 pencil was used for the lightest area in the lower portion.

Figs. 175 and 176. The circular lines enveloping these simple shapes help to create a sense of volume. Practicing shading with simple models like these is a good way to develop your drawing technique.

lead pencil techniques

When talking about lead pencil techniques, there are some elementary, though necessary, comments that need to be made. If you draw with a clutch-type pencil, the following applies; but if you draw with a wooden pencil, I think hand sharpening (with a knife or an X-Acto) is much better because you are able to control the shape, length, and sharpness of the lead (Fig. 177). If you want to get lines as thick as the diameter of the lead, the pencil must be held in the standard way, as if for writing, slanting the pencil about 45° (Fig. 178). If you hold the pencil inside your hand, the gradient will be 30° or less. The wedge of the lead will be wider then, and so will the lines (Fig. 179). If you draw with the "back" side of the lead, you can also get fine lines (Fig. 180). Drawing with a graphite stick (see page 60, Fig. 156, G and H) and sketching with the stick in a flat position (as in Fig. 182) will give you the best shading effects. To darken a shape progressively, you have to turn the pencil every now and then, very slowly, as you are drawing (Fig. 181).

On the next page you will see some less common pencil techniques: The top row reveals the influence of the paper's texture on the final image. If you are drawing a complicated image (such as this face), and you are using a rough-grain paper, the result will be coarse and blurred looking (Fig. 184). However, if you use a fine-grain paper (Fig. 183) or are drawing a larger figure (Fig. 185), you will get a smoother look. Figs. 186 to 188 show the combined use of pencils using several gradations to create contrast and depth. The last row of drawings shows how the blending techniques (Figs. 189, 190) are capable of producing outstanding artistic quality.

Fig. 177. To sharpen pencils, you can use a pencil sharpener; however, make sure it's the kind of sharpener that gives the pencil a long cone (B), or you can use an X-Acto knife or razor blade, where you can better control the length of the lead.

Fig. 178. Note the width of the line of a lead pencil when holding it the typical way, at approximately a 45° angle.

Fig. 179. The smaller the angle of the pencil in relation to the paper, the wider the resulting line.

Fig. 180. If you turn the pencil perpendicular to the paper, you can obtain lines as fine as these.

Fig. 181. If you hold a graphite stick flat, the resulting stroke appears wide and uniform.

Fig. 182. To intensify lines while drawing, there is no method better than slowly turning the drawing instrument on its side.

Fig. 183. This drawing has been made with a soft 2B pencil on a high-quality glossy paper. This type of paper has an almost unnoticeable grain, which gives the shaded areas a tonal uniformity even though they have not been blended.

Fig. 184. The same drawing made with a soft 2B pencil, but on a medium-grain paper (also high-quality) will present this imprecise finish, with gradations.

Fig. 185. When enlarging areas of the same drawing, using the same 2B pencil and medium-grain paper, the gradations are less coarse, the shapes better defined.

Fig. 186. An H pencil gives a less intense black than a 6B. By combining different grades of pencil in the same drawing, it's possible to present a range of effects and values.

Fig. 187. By playing with the white of the paper, which, in this case, is fine-grain, and using only a soft 2B pencil and an extrasoft 6B, you can achieve drawings of extraordinary contrast and energy.

Fig. 188. When blending areas made by a graphite pencil, you can use either a stump or your fingertips. Blending with fingertips is more effective and allows better control of the range of grays and intensities.

Fig. 189. Simply drawing with a lead pencil and blending for light and shade effects can be a new and exciting artistic experience, particularly in the art of the portrait.

Fig. 190. A lead pencil that has been stumped or blended can give an infinite range of value and contrast when used on high-quality glossy or smooth paper. Once the pencil has been blended it offers a uniform, harmonized finish.

Fig. 191. Lead pencil can be used effectively on colored paper when highlighted with white chalk. It's better to use a colored paper such as Canson Mi-Teintes rather than one intended for drawing with charcoal or charcoal pencil.

possibilities of the lead pencil

There are no limits to the possibilities of the lead pencil. It is the most basic and classic tool in the art of drawing. It can encompass all subjects: landscapes, urban environments, seascapes, interiors, still lifes, and portraits. But some subjects seem more appropriate than others for using the pencil; sketches, studies, and portraits come readily to mind. With the humble pencil you can sketch in the street, at home, or in nature, make composition studies, draw the live model. Look at the examples of drawing with the lead pencil on these pages to get an idea of the range possible with this most common tools.

192

Fig. 192. Landscape drawn with a soft 2B pencil and a graphite stick on glossy paper. (Actual size.)

193

194

195

Fig. 193. Urban landscape (235 x 200 mm–9 x 8 in.) drawn with H, 2B, and 6B pencils emphasizing the sense of space with lighter tones in the background and more intense darker shades in the middleground and foreground.

Fig. 194. Drypoint line drawing, made with a 2B pencil.

Fig. 195. Sketches of a head made with a 2B pencil on fine-grain paper.

196

Fig. 196. Francesc Serra. *Study*. Private collection.
This is an excellent example of a portrait made with
lead pencil. Apart from this drawing's strong sense
of form, its quality comes from combining subtly
blended areas with strong line.

charcoal and charcoal pencils

One of the earliest materials used for drawing was a burnt twig cut from vine, or a willow or a nut tree, that is: charcoal. It is a primitive drawing tool that was used by the Greeks, the Romans, and by artists in the Middle Ages and the Renaissance. In the sixteenth century fixatives were discovered, and drawing with charcoal on white or blue paper was Titian's and Tintoretto's favorite method. Guercino, in his turn, preferred to use charcoal bathed in linseed oil to get a denser and more intense black. Today artists tend to use charcoal for contour drawings, for sketching the model, for composition studies, and for sketches and preliminary drawings for finished paintings. Charcoal is useful in these cases because it can be easily erased with a piece of cloth or paper.

Fig. 197. Here are some pencils, and bars for charcoal drawings. From left to right: a chalk stick, an artificial compressed plaster similar to the pastel (1); Faber-Castell bars of artificially compressed charcoal come in six different grades (2, 3); Conté stick of artificially compressed charcoal (4); Koh-i-noor stick of charcoal and clay (5); Koh-i-noor leads of charcoal and clay that can be used with a special automatic pencil (6); charcoal pencils of different brands (A, B, C); two sizes of charcoal, which are carbonized branches of willow, grapevine, or walnut (7).

Figs. 198, 199, 200. As you will see on the following pages, charcoal, charcoal pencil, and variants of these mediums can be combined with colored pencils. These drawings are also effective when highlighted with white chalk or combined with Conté crayon.

Charcoal is available in sticks of about 6 in. (15.24 cm) in length, and the diameters range from 5 mm (1/3 in.) up to 1.5 cm (2/3 in.). Manufacturers generally produce three degrees of hardness: soft, medium, and hard. Charcoal pencil is a derivative of charcoal that is made of a charcoal lead and agglutinating substances covered with the wood of the pencil. It is also known as Conté pencil. Charcoal pencil can be found in three, four, and sometimes six gradations. These are usually distinguished by numbers or letters and come in extra soft, soft, medium, and hard.

In addition to charcoal and pencils, there are other charcoal drawing products of excellent quality. These are made of pressed charcoal or artificial coal that in some cases have been mixed with clay and agglutinizing substances

Brand	Extra Soft	Soft	Medium	Hard
Conté	3B	2B	B	HB
Faber-Castell "Pitt"	–	Soft	Medium	Hard
Koh-i-noor "Negro"	1, 2	3, 4	5	6

Fig. 201. Some manufacturers, such as Conté, offer a complete set of materials for charcoal drawing, including stumps, white chalks, sanguine pencils, compressed charcoal, white chalk, Conté crayons, and an absorbent eraser especially for charcoals.

to achieve the perfect integration of the coal (particularly in soft gradations) and the strength and density of pastels. There are also cylinder-shaped leads made with clay that produce a mat surface, which is an intense and hard-to-erase black (Fig. 197). Manufacturers produce these sticks in different gradations. Finally, there is a substance called dust charcoal, which is generally used in combination with chalks or pressed charcoal and is meant to be blended with stumps and fingertips.

200

201

202

Fig. 202. You can buy powdered charcoal to use only with a stump, or combined with black or white chalk. This combination can be made also with colored clay and chalks of the same colors.

charcoal and charcoal pencils

The greatest drawback when using charcoal, and to some extent this is true of charcoal pencil, is that it is difficult to keep the point sharp, which forces you to draw less precisely and often on a larger scale; you can't draw miniatures with charcoal. The studies of figures made with charcoal are usually made on sheets of paper 14 × 20 in. (35 × 50 cm). The imprecise properties of charcoal also make it a much freer and looser medium than the lead pencil (see examples on pages 74 and 75). The larger scale and freer realization also determines the way charcoal should be held (see Figs. 203, 204, 205).

Charcoal and charcoal pencils are particularly suitable for studies, for modeling light and shade effects, and for creating volume. Therefore, it is useful for the artist to choose models and lighting conditions that take advantage of charcoal's special properties. Keep in mind that in most art schools, a typical project includes the rendering of sculptures with either charcoal or charcoal pencil. As you will see later in the practice chapter, the use of the stump and fingertip blending is particularly important when undertaking assignments of this sort.

Charcoal is easily erasable. If you rub a piece of cloth or paper against the paper, the mark disappears, though not completely. If the stroke was intense, a slight residue of charcoal, difficult to erase even with a plastic eraser will remain on the paper. Because of the volatile nature of both charcoal and charcoal pencils, it's necessary to fix the drawing once it has been completed. Fixatives are nothing more than a coat of sprayed liquid, which, after drying, forms a film that covers and protects the drawing. Fixatives are sold in bottles and atomizers. Drawings can also be fixed with a mixture of sugar, water, and alcohol sprayed with a hand pump or with hair spray. However, the safest and most practical way of fixing is with an atomizer devised for this purpose.

Fig. 203. Because charcoal is unstable, you can't lean or rub against a charcoal drawing. To avoid smudging the surface, you should draw with the tip of the charcoal away from your hand, as shown in this illustration.

Fig. 204. For applying broad tonal areas, the best technique is to break a piece of charcoal and use it on its side to achieve the wide, uniform lines shown in the illustration.

Fig. 205. By drawing with the flat side of a piece of charcoal, but skimming it lightly over the paper, you can achieve lines of great charm and spontaneity.

Fig. 206. A manual spray fixative liquid is sprayed out of a tube bent at a right angle (A). Note that in B, the drawing has been placed on the inclined top of a table and then sprayed with fixative.

Fig. 207. When using an aerosol fixative, place the drawing on an inclined board, or hold the container up in the air as you spray. In any case, spraying with a fixative must be done progressively, step by step, using two or three coats. Remember to wait for the first one to dry before applying the second one.

Fig. 208. Charcoal can be easily erased. By brushing your finger over a charcoal line, you will lift most of the charcoal powder, smudging the line. Even if you blow an area blackened with charcoal, part of the powder will disappear, which reduces the value of the area (C, D). If you pass a clean finger through a black charcoal area, your finger will pick up the charcoal, creating a stripe of less intensity that is clearly lighter (E). Finally, if you rub vigorously with a cloth on this charcoal spot, the rag will remove all the charcoal, smudging the adjacent areas and leaving just the faintest trace of tone. This faint gray tone can be removed somewhat with an eraser, but you can never get back the absolute white of the paper (F).

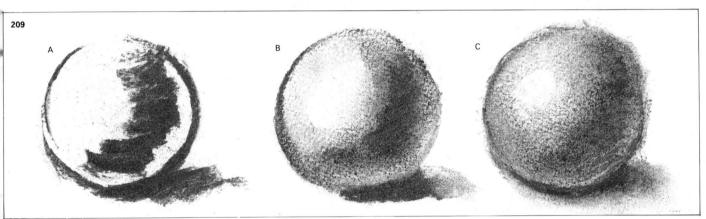

Fig. 209. Drawing a sphere with charcoal. Charcoal is an ideal way to combine the speed of a pencil with light and shade capabilities. To demonstrate, let's draw a sphere: in the first step (A), I draw the outline and fill in two areas with dark color —the cast shadow and the shaded area on the sphere. These areas are then blended with the finger to model the sphere (B). In C, I have reinforced the dark and medium tones by blending them with the fingers. Reserve a clean finger to enlarge the bright area of direct light, and then reinforce the cast shadow by blending its edges. For a final touch, I highlight the area struck by direct light by using en asborbent eraser.

Fig. 210. Usefulness of an absorbent eraser. By molding an eraser into a cone shape or a pencil-point shape you can draw small, detailed forms such as shown here. On the right (B), an area filled in with charcoal and then erased vigorously will not disappear completely but will leave a light gray tone.

Fig. 211. A gradation created by a charcoal pencil (A), when blended, will darken and lose the original tone (B). To achieve a subtle gradation like the one in figure A, lay in a smaller area with the charcoal pencil, and then spread it with the stump or the fingertips (C, D). This will confirm the idea that, in general, blending intensifies charcoal markings.

According to the historian Heinrich Wölfflin, art in the Western Hemisphere underwent a change during the Baroque period in the seventeenth century. At this time, the emphasis in art became less linear, and forms became more modeled and were rendered by means of massing and light and shade effects. Charcoal is an ideal medium for attaining these effects; it is possible actually to "paint" while drawing in charcoal through shading or massing. You only need to take a piece of charcoal and sketch some lines with it in a zigzag fashion or darken the paper to see how easy it is to make your lines wider or in subtle shades of gray. Or, you can increase the pressure until you arrive at a real blackness and rub your fingertip against the paper, and paint!

Figs. 212 and 213 (left). José Parramón. *Sketch for a Portrait.* Charcoal pencil and white chalk on colored paper. (above) Francesc Serra. *Head Study.* Charcoal. Both drawings are good examples of the potential of charcoal to capture from with massing and light and shade. In the drawing by Serra, with the exception of the line that defines the check at the left, everything else is created with values and masses. In the sketch on the left, the pictorial concept is confirmed by the lost-and-found edges, but also by the lack of color and the use of highlighting to bring out form and pull out the lights.

Figs. 214, 215, 216. José Parramón. Here are three different charcoal drawings. In the still life, I have worked and blended the charcoal with the fingers, darkening it later with a charcoal pencil. In the sketch of one of the entrances to the Plaza Mayor in Madrid, I drew in charcoal without blending. In the drawing of Venus di Milo, I began by indicating where the light and shade effects would go with the charcoal. I then erased the charcoal with a rag, and over that base, I drew in the rest of the drawing with charcoal and created its shaded areas with the stump and the fingertips.

216

chalks and sanguines

One hundred and fifty million years ago a great portion of the earth was under the sea. Fish, molluscs, and many other organisms developed there. Seventy million years later the so-called orogenic movements made the land emerge from the water. In some areas, layers of limestone of organic origin appeared. These layers were soft, white, and gray, and are still visible in many places. Many of these layers contain fossils of that period, which is known to geologists as the Cretaceous Age.

Chalk is a kind of limestone which is made into sticks by mixing white chalk with water and some agglutinating substances (Fig. 217: 1, 4, and 8). It is used to enhance white areas on a charcoal or sanguine drawing.

Chalk comes in different colors. For pure colors it is made up of color pigments, and for intermediate colors it is mixed with white chalk. Chalk manufacturers, who some years ago only used to make five or six different colors (white, gray, dark sienna, ultramarine blue, and black) have expanded their selection with twelve, twenty-four, thirty-six, and even seventy-two different colors! Some manufacturers such as Koh-i-noor, which produces twelve and twenty-four color boxes, still call them chalks; others, such as Rembrandt, which makes fifteen, thirty, forty-five, sixty, ninety, and one hundred-eighty color boxes, label them pastels.

However, even though such a range of colors is now available, the chalks most frequently used in drawing are still the original colors: sanguines, dark sienna, blue, black, and white.

Fig. 217. Here we have a selection of sanguine chalks and pencils. From left to right: white, dark sienna, and sanguine Conté crayon (1, 2, 3); white and sanguine Koh-i-noor leads of a 5 mm diameter (4, 5); and a sanguine, dark sienna and white Conté pencils (6, 7, 8).

Fig. 218. Some years ago the range of oil crayons and oil pastels was limited: just two or three siennas, plus a sanguine, a dark blue, and a dark green. These colors were enough to create high-quality drawings on colored paper highlighted with white chalk. Today, however, manufacturers have increased the number of colors up to sets of 12, 24, 36, and 72.

Figs. 219, 220, 221 (opposite page). Jean-Antoine Watteau (1684-1721). *Figure for Springtime.* Charcoal, sanguine, and white chalk on cream paper. Jean-Baptiste Greuze (1725-1805). *Head of a Young Woman.* Pastel, sanguine, and white chalk on red-tinted paper. Louvre, Paris. Jean-Antoine Watteau. *Study of a Young Woman.* Sanguine with charcoal and white chalk on gray paper. Albertina Museum, Vienna. Highlighting the lights with white chalk is a technique as old as paper dying. Later Leonardo da Vinci applied white chalk to sanguine drawings and in some of his later work to pencil, ink, and charcoal drawings. In the eighteenth century, most artists drew with mixed media. Watteau, for example, drew *à trois crayons* (drawing in three pencils), by which he meant: charcoal pencil, sanguine, and white chalk.

218

Sanguine is made up of iron oxide with some chalk. It was first used for drawing by the year A.D. 1500, and historians agree that Leonardo da Vinci was the first artist to use it. Today sanguine can be found in the form of Conté crayons and pencils, in two or three color variants (Fig. 217: 3, 5, 6, and 7).

Artists began to use white chalk as an enhancer at the beginning of the fifteenth century, when the use of paper–either white or tinted–was becoming commonplace. Botticelli, Di Credi, Lippi, Perugino, Verrocchio and others have left examples of this technique applied to drawings made with a metalpoint. But when Leonardo began to draw with sanguine on cream-colored paper, most artists of that period began to use the combination of sanguine (or charcoal), colored paper, and white chalk enhancements. That formula reached its heyday in the eighteenth century with Fragonard, Boucher, and particularly with Watteau, who popularized *le dessin à trois crayons*; that is, the combination of charcoal pencil, sanguine, and white chalk on cream-colored paper.

Then, as now, sanguine drawings, with or without white chalk, need to be fixed.

220

219

221

combined techniques

222

223

224

Fig. 222. Jean-Antoine Watteau (1684-1721). *Study of a Nude*. Black chalk and sanguine on cream paper. Louvre, Paris. Sanguine, or Conté crayon as it is known today, on cream paper is an excellent way to represent the color of flesh. You can achieve a perfect result with this medium by reinforcing some areas with black chalk or charcoal pencil.

Fig. 223. François Boucher (1703-1770). *Youngster with a Rose*. Black chalk, sanguine, and pastel on ochre-gray paper. This drawing is an inspired example of the potential inherent in combining various media.

Fig. 224. Peter Paul Rubens (1577-1640). *Portrait of Isabel Brandt*. Charcoal pencil, sanguine, and white chalk on a light sienna paper. The drawing of the eyes has been emphasized with a pen and India ink. By using only sanguine and charcoal and later highlighting with white chalk, Rubens has obtained color nuances that are really extraordinary. This is a masterful lesson on the possibilities offered by paper that is similar in color to flesh and then combined with the richness of mixing a single color with black and white.

225

The means for drawing are many and varied: lead pencil, charcoal, charcoal pencil, compressed charcoal bars, pastels, pen and ink, reed pen, ballpoint pen, felt-tipped pen, Rapidograph, or India ink washes. It is no wonder that with this diversity of methods, the artist will try to mix techniques to enrich the work. There is no doubt that the possibilities of these mixed techniques are extraordinary, as you can see in the examples on these pages.

Fig. 225. Badia Camps. *Study of Figure*. Private collection. Black, gray, and colored pastels. This drawing is an example of the possibilities of pastel as a drawing medium.

drawing with pen and ink

The oldest method of drawing with black or sepia-colored inks is the reed pen. But by the year A.D. 600, codices were written in ink with a reed pen, made of bamboo cane. Dürer used the reed pen for drawing and so did Van Gogh and Matisse, but most of Rembrandt's outstanding drawings were made with a quill made from goose, swan, or crow feathers. By the end of the eighteenth century, the first metallic pen, or "Perry," appeared. It was named after its inventor, the Englishman James Perry.

The reed pen, the quill pen, and by the nineteenth century, the metallic pen were the only tools known and used for drawing with India ink, which was invented about 2,500 years B.C. However, in the twentieth century, drawing with a pen suggests a range of about twelve different kinds of pens that in general produce a drawing in black or dark ink applied to white paper, with very little tonal gradation. A sampling of the variety of pens and inks available is shown below.

Black India ink can be found in solid form, made into sticks, or in liquid form, kept in flasks and bottles. The stick form of India ink is used for wash drawings made with a brush, whereas liquid India ink is used for drawing with metallic pen, brush, or reed pen. Inks are also available in different colors, among them: sepias and siennas for pen and wash drawings; soluble white ink for making small white shapes enhancing drawings with white. There are also other types of ink, such as blue inks for fountain pens and black and colored inks for drawing pens and technical pens.

The classic drawing pen is the metallic nib, which can be adapted to a wooden handle. You can use different types of metallic nibs with the same handle: flat-bodied, flat-tipped, round-tipped, and so on. The Graphos Company manufactures a type of handle with a small container for ink and about seventy differently shaped nibs. Some people draw with an Osmiroid fountain pen, which contains a special cartridge for ink.

As you can see in Fig. 226, the brushes most widely used are those made of sable (5), mongoose (6), size n°. 3 to 6. For special effects, rubbings, pointillist effects, and so forth, you can use a brush of pig bristle (7), or a Japanese sumi-e-style brush for wash painting (8). Black ballpoint pens are a good tool for continuous line drawings; but the ideal tool for this type of regular line of constant thickness is the technical pen. Technical pens have the advantage of coming with independent ink cartridges. They can be used with a great variety of nibs, ranging from a very fine (size 6×0) to a relatively wide line (size 7). Felt-tip pens can also be used to achieve a distinct style of pen drawing. They are available in three tip sizes: fine, medium, and broad.

Fig. 226. Today there are different materials and tools that allow us to enrich ink drawing techniques. From left to right: An India ink bar that is meant to be dissolved in distilled water and applied with a paintbrush (1). Liquid India ink used for drawing with a pen, brush, or reed pen (2). A Perry-type metal nib with a drawing handle, and (above) three kinds of pens in everyday use (3, A, B, C). An ordinary fountain pen used for drawing with blue ink, not suitable for black India ink (4), although there is a fountain pen made especially for drawing with India ink called an Osmiroid. Brushes for drawing with black or colored India ink: sable, mongoose, bristle, Japanese, and deer hair (5, 6, 7, 8). A black ballpoint pen (9). A Rapidograph for drawings that require lines of a constant thickness; it is sold with nibs for drawing lines as fines as 0.13 mm and as thick as 2.00 mm (10). Felt-tipped pens: fine point, medium point, and thick point (11, 12, 13). A black colored pencil (14). A reed pen (15). Burnt sienna India ink (16). A white India ink soluble in water (17). A china palette with wells where you can dissolve India ink (bar or liquid, black or colored inks) in distilled water.

226

Fig. 227. This ink drawing was made with a Perry-type metal nib. There are no continuous medium values here, but you can obtain tonal gradations by laying in series of lines.

Fig. 228. Vincent van Gogh. *The Garden at St. Paul's*. India ink. Van Gogh did this drawing with ink, occasionally wetting the pen in distilled water, or in sepia diluted with water, in order to create lighter color values. A neglected garden such as this one was a valuable subject for Van Gogh. In a letter to his brother Theo, he said: "This desolate garden, with all these pine trees under which the grass and the weeds grow tall and neglected, has been good enough for me to work."

227

228

16

Fig. 229. Albrecht Dürer. *Praying Hands*. Black and white ink on blue paper. Albertina Museum, Vienna. Note the use of white ink in this drawing.

Fig. 230. In this detail of a drawing made with India ink and a reed pen, note the variety of line widths and values that the reed pen is capable of producing.

229

230

17

18

10   11   12   13   14   15

techniques of pen drawing

How to hold the pen. A pen can be held in the normal way when you want to draw fine or medium-sized lines.

The pen should be held more slanted to draw thick horizontal or diagonal lines

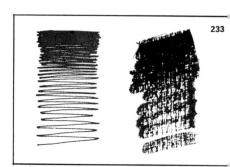

Paper for ink drawings. A high-quality, glossy drawing paper is an excellent surface for drawing in ink using any type of pen. A rough, medium-grain paper is a good choice when you want to emphasize the effects of drybrush and the reed pen.

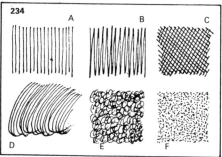

Pen strokes drawn with a metal pen or Rapidograph. Note the effect of pen strokes made with separated lines (A); zigzag lines (B); crosshatched lines (C); curving lines (D); little circles (E); and, simply, a grouping of dots (F).

Pen strokes drawn with a reed pen, a drybrush, and a black colored pencil. In the following examples, I used a rough, medium-grained paper.

Tonal gradations. From left to right: A gradation made with a metal nib, initiated with thick zigzag lines and finished with separated fine lines; series of fine parallel lines thickened and gradated with the metal nib; crosshatching made with a reed pen.

Metal pen. This illustration shows you the possibilities of creating several values and a sense of space with a metal nib. Note how the contour lines serve to envelop and define the forms.

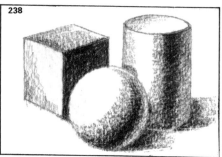

Black colored pencil. The black colored pencil, black wax pencil, and black lithographic pencil work well on fine- or medium-grain paper. This loose, sketchy style of drawing offers many possibilities for creating fully realized drawings.

Pen and graphite pencil. When combining these two mediums, begin by modeling the form with a pencil. Then with the Rapidograph pen, trace a series of identical parallel lines. Finally, use the metal nib to intensify the initial pencil shadings.

Metal pen and drybrush on fine-grained paper. Note the possibilities of drybrush applied on a drawing where a metal nib has been already used to highlight some contours. Note also the direction of the contour lines and the pen strokes that define and envelop the forms. In this drawing, metal nib pen strokes are subtle in comparison to the bolder drybrush lines.

Graphite pencil on glossy paper. This drawing was initially developed with modeling and shading and later tonal areas were created by dots, a technique known as pointillism.

242

243

244

Masking fluid, graphite pencil, and washes. Masking fluid is a product that enables you to reserve white areas of your drawing when painting in washes of ink or watercolor. In this case, the drawing has been stained with a wash of India ink. This method of staining

is done by saturating a piece of bristol board with India ink and then pressing it to the drawing so that the ink is transferred to the drawing by pressure. Depending on the amount of pressure and the quantity of the ink, you get various shades of gray, from very dark to very light.

The masking fluid can be removed with a soft eraser, and later you can define some forms with the Rapido-graph, and paint other areas with a wash of India ink.

245

246

247

248

Reserving white areas with masking fluid. The masking fluid used in watercolor to reserve white areas of the paper can be also used to reserve white areas when you are drawing with India ink. The process is the same: once the major shapes have been drawn in, you

fill in the white areas with the masking fluid. You can then paint over the reserved areas with the ink wash. Finally, you erase the masking fluid and retouch small areas with a metal nib.

Reserving white areas with white India ink. Small white shapes, such as dots and lines, can be drawn over black India ink once it is dry. The finish of these reserved areas is not as clean and hard-edged as the ones reserved with masking fluid.

249

250

251

Ink line drawing. A line drawing has no tonal areas and is solely developed with regular and constant lines. It's best done with a graphite pencil, a ballpoint pen, or a fine-line felt-tipped pen.

White ink on dark colored paper. On a black or dark-colored paper, you can use white soluble ink to create the lights and shades of a drawing. Paint in the light areas with white ink, leaving the shaded and dark areas to be formed by the dark color of the paper.

Imitating a boxwood engraving with drawing. On a special bristol board called grattage by Canson, you can draw in negative shapes by painting the board with black India ink and then scratching in white lines with a well-sharpened lancet.

252

253

254

Ink drawing in a blocked style. This is a style in which there are no halftones, only black masses defining the forms. You can draw with a brush and India ink, but the results are better with black gouache.

Finger painting. This is done by rubbing your fingers over a wet wash in order to achieve soft blurred forms and lines. In finger painting, you need to study the degree of moisture over which you apply the wash. You can use India ink and distilled water or watercolor and ordinary tap water.

Japanese wash: Sumi-e. Sumi-e is a Japanese ink drawing technique that requires special training. It is done with India ink and a bamboo brush on fine-grain watercolor paper.

drawing with a reed pen

At first sight, with its dark, medium, and light grays, a drawing by reed pen may look like one made with lead pencil. But on closer inspection the strokes you see do not have a gloss, the blacks are mat, and, as a general rule, the drawing has an intensity and strength characteristic of India ink.

When you draw with a reed pen, the amount of pressure you exert on it is the main determinant of the degree of tonal gradation you get. Of course, it's not possible to get a light gray such as the one of the mountain on this page if the reed is taken directly from the ink-pot and is excessively loaded.

To use the reed correctly, you first immerse it in the ink and tap off the excess ink on the ink-pot rim; experiment with strokes on a scrap piece of paper until you get the gradation or value intensity you want; and then go immediately to the actual drawing. A word of advice: The scrap testing paper should be of the same kind and quality as the original, otherwise you won't be able to duplicate the effect you want. The reed pen is basically a simple technique. To succeed in this medium, you just need to practice until you have a good command of the more-or-less ink and more-or-less pressure game. In spite of this, you'll find that you won't always achieve a perfect uniformity and regularity, but so much the better: Small accidents and little imperfections are often just the thing to give a certain sparkle to a work of art.

Fig. 255. The reed pen is a drawing instrument available in art supply stores. However, you can make one yourself by using a common reed or an old paintbrush handle, tapering it at one end to a point, and making a small incision or cut at the end to hold the ink.

Fig. 256. When drawing with the reed pen, you should have on hand a scrap piece of drawing paper of the same quality as the one being used, in order to discharge the excess ink that could be in the reed and to control the intensity of the lines.

Fig. 257. This drawing was made on glossy paper. To begin, I filled in with dark color the basic shapes and later put in the intermediate tones.

Fig. 258. Notice in the finished drawing the variety of line thicknesses. These differences were created by position of the reed pen in relation to the paper surface. Also notice the different directions of the pen strokes: horizontal for the mountains in the background, diagonal for the rooftops, and vertical for the walls.

255

256

257

brushes and india ink

Jesús Blasco, a good friend of mine, who is a well-known illustrator in Europe, used to say, "Brushes are a most plastic tool. They make you feel more at ease." Blasco paints with sable brushes nos. 2 and 3 for linear strokes, and with a nº. 5 for washes and background tone. He uses Canson glossy paper.

Brushes and India ink make a very good drawing combination. For example, with brush and ink, you can use the drybrush technique, which consists of rubbing the brush with scarcely any ink against the paper. This technique will give you brushstrokes of varying values, depending on the amount of ink and pressure exerted. Of course, the paper you use must be either fine or medium grain. A fine texture is indicated for small format drawings, but larger drawings require medium-grain papers. The papers should be of good quality, well glued, so that its grain is textured enough to pick up the small amount of ink on the brush.

Fig. 259. This drawing was done on fine-grain paper, its grain size slightly larger than the one in Fig. 261. I worked with sable brushes, nº. 8 and 4. As with the reed pen, you also need to have a piece of scrap paper to discharge the excess ink and to test the tones and intensities before beginning the final drawing.

Fig. 260. It is important to compose the basic structure of the model's face with the major shaded areas. I did this with medium-grade pencil–an HB– and then redrew the features with India ink and a nº. 4 brush.

259   **260**

Figs. 261 and 262. Light gray tonal areas can be achieved by a brush that is half dry. To get darker grays, intensify them progressively with several applications of the brush. First draw the contour lines of the model, not only the internal ones but also the external. Then, to create a sense of volume, use a wetter brush to fill in with softer gradations of tone; this will serve to soften the hardness of the contour lines.

262

colored pencils

Drawing-painting with colored pencils is in fashion now. I use the term *drawing-painting* because when you work with colored pencils you are not only drawing, you are making tonal gradations, mixing colors, contrasting colors, experimenting with colors–in a word, painting. Drawing with colored pencils is a fine way of getting started in the art of painting.

263

264   1   2   3   4   5

Fig. 263. This metal box comes with two tray sets of 72 pencils, made by Rexel Cumberland. Also available are a set of 24 water-soluble pencils and a set of 72 color "all in color" sticks.

Fig. 264. From left to right are five colored pencils: (1) a Derwent Studio red pencil made by Rexel-Cumberland; (2) a Faber-Castell colored pencil; (3) a school-quality pencil made in Germany by Staedtler; (4) a soft water-soluble Prismalo II pencil made by Caran d'Ache; (5) and a school-quality pencil made by Talens-Rembrandt.

Fig. 265. Below is the sixty-color pencil set made by Faber-Castell. Note the great range of colors and subtlety of tones. Recently, Faber-Castell has introduced to the market a thirty-six color set of water-soluble colored pencils.

265

The lead of a colored pencil consists of colored pigments agglutinated with a special type of wax and some varnish; then the compressed ingredients are protected with a layer of cedarwood. Standard-quality colored pencils can be found in twelve-color boxes. But for the purposes of the artist, the high-quality colored pencils are recommended. They come in metallic boxes of twelve, twenty-four, thirty-six, forty, sixty, and seventy-two pencils. Caran d'Ache manufactures a maximum range of forty colors. Berol offers a range of sixty (see them at the bottom of this page). The English brand Rexel Cumberland has a top range of seventy-two different colors. These manufacturers also provide additional colors.

Some brands of colored pencils make a distinction between those that are water resistant and those that are water soluble. Caran d'Ache colors are water soluble, and they are made in two different gradations: Supracolor I, and a softer one, Supracolor II. Faber has recently put on the market the Albrecht Dürer "watercolorable" pencils, in boxes of twelve, twenty-four, and thirty-six colors. Rexel Cumberland offers, in addition to its box of forty-two water-soluble pencils, the novelty of square-shaped leads of different colors, without wood protection. These new leads measure 5/16 × 4 in. (8 mm × 12 cm) long and are covered with lacquer to prevent their rubbing off on one's fingers. They are perfect for backgrounds and large tonal areas, and are manufactured in seventy-two different colors, though they can be bought in special ranges of twelve colors, classified as bright, shade, and pastel colors.

Figs. 266 and 267. Is it better to sharpen pencils with a knife or with a pencil sharpener? Although there is no unanimous opinion on this subject, it seems more practical, quicker, and cheaper (the pencil lead doesn't break so easily) to use a good pencil sharpener so long as it gives you a long cone.

Fig. 268. Holding only one pencil at a time is usually not a practical way to work with colored pencils. Also if you leave your pencils scattered on a work table, you risk damaging them. It's a better idea to hold all pencils you need in one hand as you draw with the other hand.

Fig. 269 (above). A pencil should not be held at too wide an angle from the paper; this position runs the risk of breaking the pencil lead.

Fig. 270. High-quality colored pencils can be expensive, so you should make the most of them. When they get too short to hold by hand use a metal pencil holder.

270

a lesson in color from van gogh

From the age of nineteen until his death, Van Gogh wrote 256 letters to his brother Théo. The last one (undated) was found on his body July 29, 1890, after he had committed suicide at the age of thirty-seven. His brother Théo died six months later.

The well-known book *Letters to Théo,* which has been translated into many languages, is about Van Gogh's private drama, his loneliness, and his anxiety. But it also deals with his ideas, his knowledge, and his achievements in drawing and painting. One of the most interesting and informative of Van Gogh's ideas to be found in the letters is on his theory of color: "There are only three colors which are truly elementary in nature and which, when they are mixed two at a time, produce three more compound colors which may be called *secondary.*"

As an illustration of Van Gogh's theory, look at the three primary colors on this page: yellow, blue, and red (Fig. 271). These three col-

271

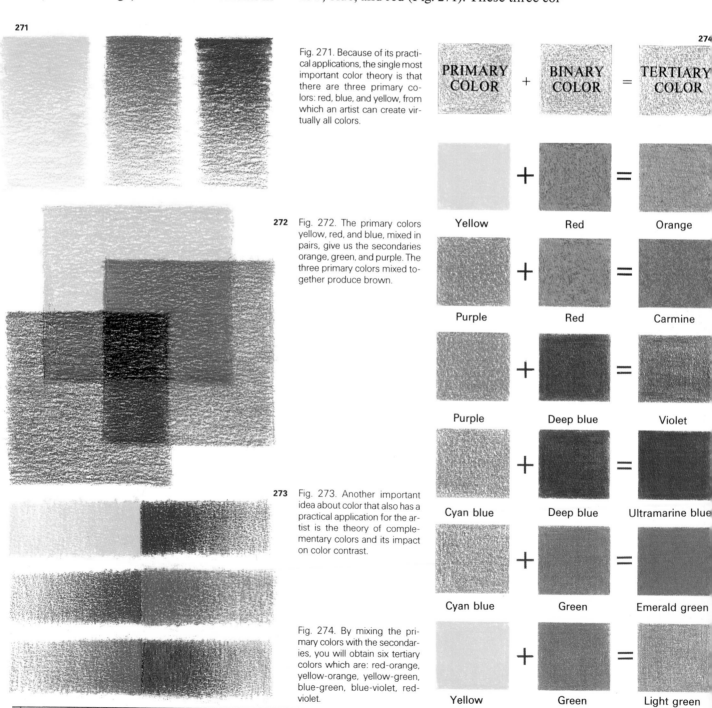

Fig. 271. Because of its practical applications, the single most important color theory is that there are three primary colors: red, blue, and yellow, from which an artist can create virtually all colors.

272

Fig. 272. The primary colors yellow, red, and blue, mixed in pairs, give us the secondaries orange, green, and purple. The three primary colors mixed together produce brown.

273

Fig. 273. Another important idea about color that also has a practical application for the artist is the theory of complementary colors and its impact on color contrast.

Fig. 274. By mixing the primary colors with the secondaries, you will obtain six tertiary colors which are: red-orange, yellow-orange, yellow-green, blue-green, blue-violet, red-violet.

274

PRIMARY COLOR	+	BINARY COLOR	=	TERTIARY COLOR
Yellow	+	Red	=	Orange
Purple	+	Red	=	Carmine
Purple	+	Deep blue	=	Violet
Cyan blue	+	Deep blue	=	Ultramarine blue
Cyan blue	+	Green	=	Emerald green
Yellow	+	Green	=	Light green

ors mixed together "beget," as Van Gogh used to say, the three secondary colors: orange, green, and violet (Fig. 272).

If you look at the right hand column (Fig. 274) you will see how to compose the six tertiary colors by mixing one primary and one secondary. From top to bottom these are: orange, carmine, violet, ultramarine, emerald green, and light green.

To prove this theory to yourself, there is no better medium than colored pencils to experience that:

All the colors in nature can be composed by mixing the three primary pigment colors: yellow, red, and blue.

Van Gogh also talks about complementary colors and says that when two primary colors (yellow and blue, for instance) are mixed, the result (green) is the complement of the primary that did not take part in the mixture (red). Thus, we can say with Van Gogh that:

Purple is the complement of yellow

Orange is the complement of blue

Green is the complement of red

But, you may ask, what is the use of knowing what the complementary colors are? Van Gogh's answer to this question is the same as any experienced artist's. A knowledge of color theory helps you to:

Create contrasts: The juxtaposition of two complementaries, says Van Gogh, "will increase their intensity so much that the human eye will hardly be able to bear it."

Paint with broken colors: "If two complementary colors are mixed in unequal amounts the result will be a broken color, or a variety of gray." (This rule applies when you are drawing-painting with colored pencils or watercolors.)

As an epilogue to this short lesson, try drawing-painting any subject with only three primary colors (and perhaps black). I have done this exercise using eleven colors and black and with three colors (and black). The result is obvious if you look at Figs. 275, 276. Why then, you may wonder, do manufacturers sell boxes with 60, and even 72 different colors?

Let me show you the answers on the following pages.

275

276

Figs. 275 and 276. Using only the three primary colors plus black and white, it is possible to compose all the colors in nature. For example, the head drawn above was painted using eleven colors plus black and white. The head below was painted with only the three primary colors, plus black and white. As you can see, the result is not identical but acceptable, and it confirms in practice the basic precepts of color theory.

drawing/painting with colored pencils

Use colored pencils for preliminary drawings. Use light blue, light gray, or light sienna, depending on the amount of cool, neutral, or warm colors offered by the model. Never use a lead pencil because pencil marks remain visible against the subsequent color application.

Use the white of the paper for white areas of the drawing. Usually the white of the paper acts as white color in a drawing. White colored pencils are not effective because they are neither opaque or capable of covering colors.

Color mixing by superimposing colors. With modern sets of 40 pencils, you can always choose to use one color to create the direct color you want. However, subtle color changes and nuances are best achieved by superimposing one color over another.

Build up color gradually. As you can see in this step-by-step example, colored pencil technique is developed by a progressive build-up of color.

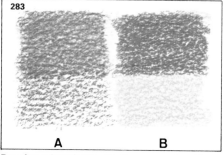

Practice color mixing with the same colors. Over a gray-blue tonal area, I have superimposed yellow to obtain a light green (A). By changing the order of the colors, that is, starting with the yellow and then superimposing blue, the resulting green is darker (B).

Pastel color effects. The cube and the cylinder of the above drawing (284, 285) were drawn, at first, with the same pencils and colors, but later, in the figure on the right, I used a white colored pencil over the blue in the

background, the rosy planes of the cube, the shadow projected by the cube on the cylinder, and the light reflected by the cylinder. The whitish patina achieved here is similar to the soft look of a pastel drawing.

The size and texture of colored pencil paper. A colored pencil drawing is usually not large. Either 20 x 25 cm (8 1/2 by 10 in.) or 25 x 30/35 cm (10 x 12/14 in.) are advisable sizes. It is also recom-

mended that the grain of the paper should be related to the size of the drawing: For a large work, a fine or medium grain (Fig. 286) paper works well; for a small work, use a paper with a very fine texture (Fig. 287).

Colored pencils on colored paper. Colored papers, such as cream, light blue, gray, or salmon, make a wonderful surface for drawing-painting with colored pencils. They help to harmonize the color and allow you to highlight the whites with white pencil.

Color theory and practice. This scale of colors of the sprectrum (left) was developed by using the three primary colors. The spectrum in the next figure (right) was drawn with twelve different pencil colors. It is obvious that in the righ thand picture there is a greater richness and diversity of color. For example, compare the range of greens, blues, purples, and violets you see, and you'll come to the conclusion that more colors will give you better results.

Water-soluble colored pencils vs. watercolor. In the examples, compare the quality of water-soluble colored pencils with swatches of real watercolor. In Fig. 291, you can see a toned area filled in with a blue pencil (A), and then the same area after it has been dissolved with a brush charged with water (B). Swatch was created by using a blue watercolor wash. (C) This gradation was drawn in with a dark carmine pencil and later dissolved with water (D), and here I have painted the same carmine colored gradation with watercolor (E). Note that the watercolor swatches are cleaner and more transparent than are colored pencils combined with water.

The wash technique using a water-soluble colored pencil. This is a very helpful technique, used primarily for small washes and made with a single color. It is even easier than a simple watercolor wash.

The importance of line direction. As I have said before, you can paint as well as draw with colored pencils. When you draw, however, the lines created are distinctive. These lines are the most important element in determining and developing the forms of your drawing. For example, if you are drawing the sea, lines will tend to be horizontal, or if you are drawing a field of grass, lines typically will be short and vertical.

The colored pencil as an auxiliary medium. In contemporary illustration, as demonstrated in this picture by Maria Rius (Fig. 294) the watercolor medium is perhaps the most commonly used. However, pastel and colored pencil are often used for finishing touches. In this case, colored pencil can be found in the girl's hair.

Colored pencil finishing of marker drawings: Light colored pencils, such as yellow, white, pink, are usually applied over dark areas of drawings done with markers to represent fog or, as in this case, the effects of a geyser (Drawing by Claude de Seynes).

A subject such as you see here with this range of broken colors and grays can be drawn with only three colors: yellow, purple, and cyan-blue. (In order to get a better harmonization I drew on Canson gray paper.) It is much more practical and effective to draw with direct colors, freely, without any conditions, and avoiding mixtures which, very often, do not help in getting the exact tone or the ideal color you want. Note in Fig. 297 the colors and numbers used for the seaport scene.

The last example in Fig. 297 is of white ink or possibly white gouache. White ink allowed me to enhace the drawing with a brush, a much better technique than using a white pencil. It created the brightnesss of the water in the foreground and the background, in addition to the illuminated areas of the ships, such as balustrades, masts, and so forth.

FABER CASTELL POLYCHROME COLORS USED FOR THIS SUBJECT

White, 101

Ochre, 184

Burnt ochre, 167

Burnt umber, 180

Sepia, 175

Light carmine, 127

Light blue, 146

Cobalt blue, 144

Prussian blue, 151

Silver gray, 196

Medium gray, 197

Dark gray, 198

Black, 199

White ink

297

298

299

300

Fig. 298, 299, 300. "Boats in the port of Amsterdam." On gray Canson Demi-Teintes paper, I draw this theme with a *silver gray 196* pencil and I start painting the silhouettes of the houses in the background with *sky blue 116.* With *white 101,* I highlight the sky and the water gradating from the background to the foreground, the lights on the boats, etc... Next, I proceed with the hulls and the dark reflexions of the boats on the water, first with *Prussian blue 151* and then with *dark grey 198* and *black 199.* Notice that there are small reflections left where you can see the blue. I use *medium gray 197* and *dark gray 198* in the port, behind the boats, and also *medium gray* in the foreground of the water, leaving some clear strips representing the movement of the water. *Ochre 184, burnt ochre 167, toasted umber 188,* slight touches of *carmine 127...* and finally *white ink* in the brightest brilliances, on the water in the background and foreground, on the boats, balustrades, masts, etc...

Finish with colored pencils of drawings made with felt-tipped pens. With light colored pencils: yellow, white, pink, etc... it is normal to paint over the dark areas of the drawings made with felt-tipped pens, to represent the fog, or as in this case, the effects of a geyser.

water-soluble colored pencils

301

The use of water-soluble colored pencils allows you to make gradations similar to painting and to define and to build form through pencil strokes. It also allows you to blend colors with brush and water, like painting with watercolors.

Are water-soluble colored pencils, in effect, a combined technique? Certainly! The two methods are practically inseparable. Of course, it is possible to draw-paint a subject using this kind of colored pencil as if it were not water soluble, but it is an added benefit to be able to combine the linear effects of a dry medium as pencil with the softer, liquid effects of a water medium.

In the drawing below, note the areas where pencil strokes have been blended with water (such as the sky) and the gray areas where the outlines are highlighted by the texture of the paper (such as the trees, the cars, or the land, Fig. 304).

Fig. 301 (top left). When working with colored pencil, don't use a lead pencil for a preliminary drawing because its waxy surface could come off on the color. Instead, make your preliminary sketch with a sky blue pencil. Note that in the illustration the shadow areas are sketched in with a skhy blue pencil.

Fig. 302 (middle left). This is the first stage of color before any applications of brush or water. Note that the areas intended for watercolor, such as the sky, tend to be the larger in the drawing.

Fig. 304 (below). In the finished drawing, I have used watercolor for the sky, the shadowed areas of the church, the street area, and to a lesser extent, the trees. When the watercolor areas had dried completely, I used colored pencil for the finishing details.

302

304

Fig. 304. CARAN D'ACHE WATERCOLOR COLORS AND SOFT PRISMALO II USED FOR THIS SUBJECT

ochre	035	dark green	229
khaki	249	medium gray	005
sienna	059	umbers blue	141
purple	090	sky blue	160
carmine	080	Black,	009
yellow green	245	white	001

markers

Markers are a drawing instrument commonly used today, particularly in commercial art and advertising, but also in architecture and interior design.

The marker was developed by the Japanese in the 1960s. It is a sort of fountain pen with a container inside to carry the ink to the tip. The ink is made with pigments and alcohol, or rather, xylen, a liquid very similar to alcohol. Besides permanent markers, which contain xylen, there are also water-based markers that are nontoxic and made specifically for children's use.

There are three types of markers available on the market today with three different size points: the regular nib made to fill large areas very quickly; the pointed nib, for general work; and ultrafine nib for drawing and sketching. There are several quality brands on the market including AD markers (200 colors); Design Art Markers (120 colors); Staedtler Mars Graphic 300 (60 colors); Berol Prismacolor Art Markers (116 colors); and Pantone Markers (312 colors). There is also a type of paper especially devised for drawing with markers called felt markers. However, if you can't find this type of paper you can always use a glossy-type paper, such as Bristol.

Fig. 305. In the box at right are listed five common makes of felt-tipped pens, their country of origin, and the number of colors.

WELL-KNOWN MARKERS

Manufacturer	Country of Origin	Colors Available
Ad Marker	U.S.A.	200
Eberhard Faber Design Art Markers	U.S.A.	120
Staedtler Mars Graphic 300	Germany	60
Berol Prismacolor	U.S.A.	116
Pantone		(broad tip) 204 (fine tip) 108
Letraset		

Fig. 306. Felt-tip pens are available in three versions: wide, medium, and fine tip. Notice the special design of the Magic Marker felt-tip pen, built with an inkwell from which a wick stems, that permits drawing with it, and which, if necessary, can be unscrewed so as to open the inkwell to recharge it or to use the ink with a brush.

306

307

Fig. 307. Claude de Seynes. *Louisiana house.* De Seynes is an expert on felt-tip pens. He is the author, with Jean Naudet, of a book published by Parramón Editions. De Seynes establishes in this book the following minimum assortment of felt-tip pens needed:

light yellow
intense yellow
light orange
light pink
medium red
cadmium red
mauve
light blue
vivid blue
green-blue
Prussian blue
light green
medium green
dark green
fir green
light beige or ivory
intense beige or sand
red brown
sepia
flesh
light cold gray
medium cold gray
light warm gray
medium warm gray

308

309

310

Three ways of drawing with a felt-tip pen. The wide and rectangular point of a felt-tip pen enables you to draw three line widths: a fine line made with the edge of the point (1); a medium line made with the narrower frontal side (2); and a wide line made by holding the pen at an angle (3).

Gradually from light to dark. As with watercolor painting, felt-tip pens use the paper surface for white areas. Felt-tip colors are transparent and it is not possible to superimpose a light color over a dark one. You must build up color with felt-tip pen, and develop your drawing from less color to more color and from light to dark.

311

312

313

Intensify tonal areas with the same color. The same color applied in successive coats will darken the color, as you can see in these illustrations. The one on the left has a single coat of color, and the one on the right has several applications.

Mixing color with transparent ink. The ink in felt-tip pens is transparent. Mixing colors can be done in the same way as with watercolors, by superimposing one or several coats of color or by blending the colors.

314

315

316

Draw with direct color. Although it is possible to compose one color by mixing two or more others, it is preferable, when workings with felt-tip pens, to work with the exact color. This is why manufacturers offer sets of up to 204 colors.

Drawing in background areas. As shown in the example, the typical way to lay in color with felt-tip pens is to draw in lines horizontally, diagonally, or vertically, with a wide-tip pen fast enough for the ink mark of one stroke to blend with the next one.

Achieving tonal gradations. The above gradation was created with three colors. The blending of one color with another was achieved by applying the colors in rapid succession before they were completely dry.

317

318

319

Practical applications of tonal gradations. Tonal areas were done in two stages in this example. First, horizontal lines were drawn in, reserving the white of the paper for the high-key areas. Then darker, more intense applications of color were laid in the shaded areas.

Retouching with white ink or goauche. The white circles of the top of the cup and of the plate were retouched with white ink. This is an accepted technique often practiced by artists who use felt-tip pens and markers.

Retouching felt-tip drawings with colored pencils. Illustrators often use colored pencils to outline or draw details over darker felt-tip pen drawings.

wash techniques

A wash simply means a neutral-color watercolor application. A wash drawing is made with a brush, water, and one or two neutral colors, such as black, black and sepia, or dark brown and sepia. These colors are generally watercolor pigments. However, a wash drawing can also be made with black India ink or sepia, a brush, and water, on condition that the water has been distilled, because India ink shouldn't be mixed with tap water.

Wash drawing is a necessary step before tackling watercolor painting. Wash techniques are the same as watercolor techniques with the advantage that color problems are eliminated. For example, when doing a wash drawing, you won't have to think about such problems as color mixing, color contrast, or color harmony. This is clearly an advantage: You learn the wash-technique first, and then go on to the complexity of drawing or painting with color.

In addition to wash drawing being an excellent preliminary to actual watercolor painting, wash is time-honored technique all by itself. It has been used by all the great masters–ancient and modern–from Leonardo and Michelangelo to Rubens and Rembrandt, to Van Gogh and Picasso.

Now let's tackle the wash technique in the best of all possible ways by doing it!

Fig. 320. Claude Lorrain. "Landscape with a river. View of the Tiber from Mount Mario, Rome." British Museum, London.

Fig. 321. John Constable. "Trees beside a River." Sepia Victoria and Albert Museum, London.

Fig. 322. Xu Hong. "Group of Horses." (Fragment). From the album of paintings of the artist Private Collection.

320

322

321

Begin painting from side to side, horizontally; paint with a nº. 12 brush.

Fig. 323. *Dry wash in a medium tone.* Draw a 9″ x 9″ (15 x 15 cm) square. Then, using a cobalt blue wash, wet the brush with plenty of color and begin painting a band 1″ to 1 1/4″ (2 to 3 cm) wide at the top of the square.

Now paint vertically, from top to bottom, keeping the brush loaded so that you are always painting wet-into-wet.

Fig. 324. To control the accumulation of paint and to keep it from running, the board should be slanted as necessary. Continue to maintain the moisture, working quickly. Keep displacing the wash, moving toward the bottom, painting horizontally, always leaving enough paint on the bottom edge.

Drain the brush and absorb the leftover water.

Fig. 325. Now, absorb the paint accumulated on the bottom edge of the square. To do this, blot the brush with a paper towel and absorb the paint accumulated at the bottom edge until you have a regular, uniform tone over the whole square. The uniformity in the color of a medium-dry tone wash depends on three things: the quality of the paper, the slant of the board, and the brush and the amount of paint on it.

Graded wash: Begin painting a band of intense color, from side to side, on the upper part of the square.

Fig. 326. *Dry graded wash.* Sketch a square 9″ x 9″ (15 x 15 cm) and get ready to paint a graded wash using cadmium red or vermillion in the area specified.

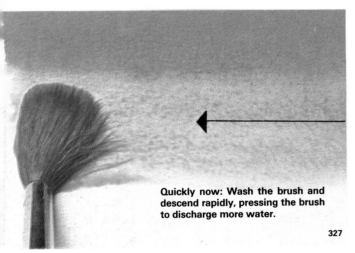

Quickly now: Wash the brush and descend rapidly, pressing the brush to discharge more water.

Fig. 327. Wash the brush, drain it slightly on the edge of water jar, and apply it to the bottom half of the red band, dissolving and gradating downward and painting from side to side horizontally. Move toward the bottom rapidly, putting pressure on the brush to release more water.

Continue moving gradually downward until you get to the bottom of the square, using whatever amount of water is necessary.

Fig. 328. Wash the brush again, and drain it, and continue controlling the amount of water going over it, retouching. You have to move quickly, measuring the water and working mainly in the bottom portion, which at this stage is the only area that allows for repeating and retouching.

wash techniques

329

Opening up white spaces by absorbing color. In wash drawing or watercolor painting, there is often the need to open up a white area in a still-wet wash. Begin by washing the brush and draining it with the

330

help of a paper towel. Apply the brush to the still wet wash area, and the brush will absorb the water and the color underneath.

331

Opening up a white area. If you want to obtain an even whiter area, apply the drained brush once again. By repeating this operation several times you can achieve an almost perfect white.

332

Dry method of opening up white areas. In a wash already dry, it is also possible to open up white areas. Begin by wetting the area with a brush and clean water. At the same time, rub gently with the brush, diluting and

333

lifting the color. Later, with a paper towel folded several times, absorb the water you applied. Repeat this operation several times until you get a satisfactory white.

334

Opening up a white area with bleach. Common bleach, watered down 50 % and applied over a dry wash, is a quick, effective way to remove pigment. But the brush must be synthetic in order to resist the corrosive action of the bleach.

335

Example: scrubbing out whites in dry paint. When you want a white in a dark area in an already-dry watercolor, it's advisable to do it with a synthetic flat brush, which has stiffer bristles than sable. Begin by moistening the chosen area with lots of water. Let the water sit for a few

336

minutes, allowing it to soften the paper and the paint, and then rub softly with a clean, rinsed brush until the deposited water begins to get cloudy with the loosened paint.

337

Begin by washing the brush and draining it with the help of a paper towel. Apply the brush to the still-wet wash area, and the brush will absorb the water and the color underneath.

338

339

340

341

Preserving white areas with masking fluid. Masking fluid is a product with which you can preserve lines, highlights, or small white areas. You apply it with a synthetic brush, and you can remove it, once it has dried, with an ordinary eraser. Note in these pictures,

from left to right, the application of the masking fluid over the initial drawing of some daisies; the later possibility of painting around and over the masking fluid without any alteration of its preserving abilities; the appearance of the drawing after the masking fluid has been

erased, showing the white of the preserved areas; and finally, the finished painting, where the preserved white becomes very convincing daisy petals.

Preserving white areas with white wax. White wax can also be used to preserve whites before you begin to paint. Once an initial drawing is completed, fill in white

areas with a white wax crayon. Then you can paint over these waxed areas because the wax will repel the watercolor pigment.

Scratching out whites in wet paint with a bevelled brush handle or a fingernail. You do this simply by scratching when the paint is still damp and the color is somewhat thick.

Textural effects with turpentine. Apply a synthetic brush loaded with turpentine over a freshly painted,

still-damp area. When the turpentine comes into contact with the watercolor, light-colored, irregularly shap-

ed spots are formed, creating special effects and textures.

Rubbing with the brush. This technique, also called *drybrush*, consists of painting with an almost dry brush, which, when rubbed, reproduces the rough texture of the paper.

Textural effects with water. A brush load with water, applied to a still-damp recently painted area will pro-

duce very rich textural effects, which will enrich the color and style of your painting.

Textural effects with salt. If you sprinkle salt on a recently painted still-damp area, the grains of salt will absorb the pigment and form some curious spots, light

in color and diffused. This effect can be used for the background areas of a watercolor, creating effects of surprising quality. When the painting is dry, the grains

of salt sticking to the painting can be removed simply by rubbing them gently with your fingers. Or you can paint over them without any problem.

wash techniques

Cube, cylinder, pyramid, and rectangle. With these four basic shapes you will carry out an exercise of wash drawing that brings to reality the previous discussion. You will need the following materials (Fig. 353):

Drawing paper for watercolor painting
A sheet of beige drawing paper (Mi-Teintes)
Paper towels
A bottle filled with water
Palette
An H pencil
Eraser
A tube of cobalt blue watercolor
A tube of burnt umber watercolor
Sable brushes n°. 8, 14
Synthetic brush n°. 12

On the facing page (Fig. 354) you will see on a small scale the patterns of the four basic shapes mentioned. For this and other exercises, it would be a good idea if you first build these models by yourself. Note also in Fig. 357 (the finished drawing) the type of lighting, the position of the various shapes, and the angle of the light. To complete the exercise, use washes of the cobalt blue and burnt umber (mentioned above) to fill in the basic shapes.

Fig. 353 (above, right): Materials and tools needed for this exercise.

Fig. 354 (following page, top): For constructing these models, use a light-weight bristol board, cutting it with a mat knife, X-acto, or razor blade. Try to cut a clean edge and follow the measurements given. It is not at all difficult to do, and you'll enjoy having the model in front of you.

356

355

Painting a still life with wash

Begin by testing, on a scrap piece of paper, the range of colors that you can obtain by mixing cobalt blue and burnt umber. You will observe that by mixing these colors, you obtain a complete range of warm, neutral, and cold grays, plus black, and a range of blues and siennas, depending on which color dominates and how much water you use.

Fig. 355. To begin, I sketch in the still life with an H pencil. With the drawing upside down, which for me is a better way to control the various gradations, I start the wash with a strong burnt umber wash for the upper part of the background and the shaded areas of the cube, the prism, and the pyramid. When this wash is dry, I fill the light-filled areas of the forms with masking fluid, and I paint with a warm dark gray, almost black, the surrounding areas. Then, I wait until the wash is dry, and finish off with a cold gray on the upper faces of the cube, the cylinder, and the prism.

Fig. 356. With a very light warm gray, I fill in the D, E, and F faces, reserving at the same time brilliances of the A, B, C edges. But note that I leave the pyramid's triangle a pure white. Once more, I must wait until the gray is dry. Then, with clean water I moisten the body of the cylinder (D) and the faces of the cube, painting wet-into-wet with color over the cylinder and its shadows that project onto the cube.

Fig. 357. With the drawing upside down again, I lay in on the cube, pyramid, and prism a very bluish gray gradated from top to bottom. When it is dry, I remoisten these areas, and lay in the shadows projected underneath the four basic forms with a warm intense gray mixed with burnt umber.

354

357

oil crayons and oil pastels

Oil crayons are basically made with pigments and wax. Oil pastels, developed about twenty years ago, are made with pigments and oil. Oil pastels are associated, as their name suggests, with pastels, a traditional medium centuries old.

But despite their differences, oil crayons and oil pastels are two methods whose possibilities and techniques are very nearly the same. Among these common features:

— Oil crayons and oil pastels are used by rubbing them against the paper. They can be blended with the fingertips.

— Both mediums are opaque, and light colors can be superimposed over dark colors.

— Both wax colors and oil pastels are difficult to erase. If you find it necessary to erase, you must first scrape off the waxy surface with a knife. After the waxy color has been scraped off, you can reapply new color without contaminating it with the first.

— If a light color is covered with a dark and a knife, or X-acto blade is scraped against the surface, the lighter color will reappear.

— Both these mediums are soluble in turpentine.

— Fixative works on both mediums.

You may wonder at this point if, in effect, these two products are really the same. Yes and no; there is a small—but important—difference: Oil crayon is harder, less malleable, and more impermeable. When you mix oil crayon colors, the resulting combination becomes stiff. It is thick, glossy, and grainless, and the pigment slides along the surface of the paper. This quality makes it necessary to scrape off the wax first before you can draw in a clean line of a light color on top. Oil pastels, on the other hand, are softer and more pliable. They allow a touch of light color on the dark one, as do real pastels.

Fig. 358. The above illustration shows Caran d'Ache's assortment of 30 Neocolor oil crayons, and a set of 45 Panda oil pastels made by Talens. Both these mediums can be dissolved in turpentine and mixed together; both can be protected with fixative.

Fig. 359. This drawing and those on the opposite page were painted on a dark brown Ingres paper. But this drawing was painted with oil crayons, while the others were done with oil pastels. When comparing these details of an old man's head, you can see that oil crayons have a harder line and more definition. On the other hand, oil pastels offer a greater opacity and a better impasto.

pastel painting techniques

Finger blending technique. Both oil pastels and oil crayons can be gently rubbed and blended with the fingers.

Covering possibilities. Here, over a dark carmine spot, I have applied a gray and white color. When using oil pastels and oil crayons, you can paint light colors over dark.

Erasing is difficult. First I fill in the area completely with dark carmine color. Then, I scratch out the area with an X-Acto which partly eliminates the color (A). Finally, I rubbed the area vigorously with an eraser (B), where, as you can see, the color has not been completely eliminated.

Drawing in negative. When applying dark color over a light, you should work slowly and carefully in order to achieve a complete covering. Once you have done this, you can scratch out the covering color to obtain initial color underneath,

Turpentine washes. Oil crayons and oil pastels can both be dissolved in turpentine, using a synthetic brush. You can then paint washes just as if you were using water-soluble colored pencils.

Painting glazes. If you dissolve oil pastel or oil crayon shavings in a little turpentine, you will get a liquid color that allows you to paint transparent glazes over your paintings. This technique works better with oil pastels.

367

Fig. 366. The initial preliminary sketch shown above was made using a white colored pencil. The finished painting was done progressively, with several layers of color. This method is a good way to develop the volume and form of the image. In this case, light color was used for the highlights and the shadowed areas are the dark brown of the Ingres paper.

Fig. 367. Techniques for oil pastels are almost the same as the ones used for oil crayons, with the notable difference that oil pastels are softer than oil crayons. This characteristic can be clearly seen in the above example drawn with oil pastels. Note the capacity of the light colors to cover, and note also the impasto effect. When applying oil pastels to paper with any pressure, you can create outstanding textures similar to some of the textures you can get from painting with oil paint. Although a certain amount of practice is necessary to achieve optimum results by this method, there is no doubt that it is worth experimenting with it as a new means of drawing-painting.

pastels

Fig. 368. Shown below is a pastel set comprised of three trays and a total of 180 colors made by Talens. Talens also offers assortments of 15, 30, 45, 60, and 90 colors. Sets are also available in colors selected especially for portraits and landscapes in boxes of 45, 60, and 90 colors.

Pastels are made up of earth and pulverized pigments agglutinated with water and gluing substances, but without the liquid base of oils, varnishes, and essences, which, in watercolor and oil painting, have an influence on the purity and richness of the color. This quality is what makes pastels somewhat fragile and unsteady. They should not be fixed (or even touched!) and, to some extent they should not even be mixed. So my advice to you is: *When working with pastel colors, use each color singly, using mixtures only to adjust values.*

Fortunately, pastel manufacturers understand this characteristic and pastels come in sets of 12, 18, 24, 36, and 48 sticks. You can also get beautiful wooden boxed sets of 99 colors (Schminke), 72 colors (Faber-Castell), and even 180 colors (Rembrandt). Rembrandt also has special sets for both portrait and landscape work; these come in sets of 46, 60, and 90 colors.

Pastels can be mixed and blended, and light colors can be painted over dark colors. In fact, fingertip blending and strokes are often alternated to get a painterly effect. Keep in mind that instead of your fingertips you could also use paper stumps, but as I have said previously, your fingertip is superior because of the natural oil in your skin. It is this oil that agglutinates and fixes pastel color.

The drawing paper used for pastel work should be medium to coarse grain. Colored paper is generally preferred, although white is acceptable. Pastels can be rubbed off with a kneaded eraser or with a piece of cloth or paper towel. Charcoal, charcoal pencils, Conté crayon, and white chalk are excellent auxiliary media to combine with pastel.

Pastels are affected by contact with moisture. If you wet a pastel stick with saliva, the intensity of the color will increase, but after a few seconds, it dries and recovers its usual color. However, if you touch pastel and have grease on your fingers, the stain remains and the color stays. Also, grease or sweat on a finger could get onto the surface you are working on. Pastel will not adhere to an oily surface. Fixatives do not contain oil, but they have some agglutinating substances that do change the refraction of light. This property darkens the colors on the one hand, but also makes them more transparent, causing them to lose their covering capabilities. Therefore, fixing a pastel drawing means losing opaqueness and luminosity. What can you do then to prevent this reaction but still be able to keep the surface of your drawing intact?

In a handbook published by Talens, the manufacturer of Rembrandt pastels, it is suggested that you fix only a few areas at a time and retouch the most affected ones later. This technique makes the fixative coating adhere better. Degas preserved his pastels by moistening the drawing paper with turpentine, which, he observed, helped to keep them.

368

It is my opinion that pastels should never be fixed, which means you must protect your drawings with a sheet of paper in such a way that it prevents contact with anything else. Then, when the drawing is completed, you will need to frame your pastel with a sheet of glass and a thick passe-partout frame to avoid contact with the glass. That is the method used by great museums to protect the work of such masters as Rosalba Carriera, Chardin, Perroneaux, Quentin de La Tour, and Degas.

369

Fig. 369. Shown here are pastel sets by Schminke (60 colors) and Faber-Castell (72 colors). Both manufacturers offer smaller assortments of 12, 24, 36 colors.

Because you can't mix pastel colors easily, a large assortment is necessary for drawing. And the wooden boxes are essential for keeping and ordering the pieces and ends of pastels. Many artists make a series of compartments inside the boxes where they classify according to color temperature warm, cool, and neutral, or according to broad areas of subject matter, such as portraits and landscapes.

pastel painting techniques

The rigid support: the board or the vertical easel. Although you can always mount your paper on cardboard and work horizontally, a pastel is best worked supported by a standard upright easel. Not only is this a better position from which to work, but it also allows the pastel dust to fall off the drawing.

Work with small pieces of pastel. A pastel artist's box contains plenty of small pieces, such as the one shown here. These pieces are perfect for making fine lines, with the pastel turned on edge, or for shading, with the pastel laid flat against the paper.

Linear and tonal qualities. When drawing fine lines with pastel, you must hold the pastel stick as if it were the end of a pencil, using the most pointed edge. To fill in tonal areas, hold the stick as shown in the picture, using the flat side of the stick.

Covering capabilities. Here, you can see how light colors, such as yellow or white, can be drawn over a darker blue or red area to give an opaque coverage, especially when applied to dark colored paper. Unfortunately, the covering quality lessens when the drawing is fixed.

Mixing and blending with the fingers. Because of the large selection of pastel colors available, you are always able to use the exact color you want. Therefore, the need to mix is lessened. Nuances of color can be achieved from a wide range of color, even within a single hue. Blending color is another matter, however. Pastels are easily blended with the fingers, but a stump might possibly be too harsh a blending tool and cause the pastel powder to loosen and crumble rather than blend.

Pastel papers: white and colors. Pastel papers can be white, but the results are often better with colored papers, where the middle value of the paper makes a good background for light and dark values, using light and dark colored pastels. The paper shown above is Canson's Mi-Teintes, an excellent paper for pastel work.

The subject can determine the color of the paper. In the case of this landscape, a green paper was an appropiate choice. When drawing a portrait or figure, however, a warm-toned paper in cream, ochre, or sienna would probably be more suitable.

Drawing papers have two sides. In actual practice, it makes very little difference which side of a pastel drawing paper you draw on. However, there are slight differences between the front and back, so the pastel artist has the advantage of choosing the most appropiate texture.

Erasing pastel. To erase an area of a pastel drawing, rub gently with a clean cloth until the area is fairly clean. You probably won't be able to remove all the pigment, but it won't be difficult to draw over it and get a good coverage.

Erasing and drawing with an absorbent eraser. Although it is very difficult to erase pastel, you can remove little details or open small white areas or lines with a malleable absorbent eraser, such as a kneaded eraser. Since this type of eraser is very soft and flexible, you can adapt it to any particular form to remove small spots of color.

The palette box. When working with a wide assortment of pastels (60 or more colors), since the breakage of the sticks creates two or three times the original number, you can understand the need for a storage box with compartments, which will allow you to classify the colors and make your work easier.

Cleaning is important. Pastel colors tend to pick up the color of other sticks. Your fingers will also get dirty from the blending that is needed in most pastel drawings. So, after use, be sure to clean up the pastel sticks and your fingers with a cloth or a paper towel.

Auxiliary mediums. Soft charcoal pencils, sanguine pencils, and particularly white chalk pencils, are perfect ways to dress up a pastel drawing and create interesting effects.

Fixatives. Fixatives tend to darken pastel colors and alter their covering capacity. Some artists maintain that it is possible to fix drawings by spraying the surface very lightly, or by spraying and then retouching the damaged color. But none of these methods is absolute or advisable in my opinion.

Protecting a pastel drawing. Since it is not advisable to fix pastel drawings, you must protect them some other way. I suggest that you cover them with a sheet of paper to avoid any rubbing or friction with other drawings or papers. Then once the drawing is finished you can frame it with a glass cover.

Framing. The fragility of pastel drawings requires a special framing technique. This technique, known as passe-partout, protects the drawing by providing a space between the drawing and the glass cover.

Pastel drawings or pastel paintings?

First in Venice, then in Paris, and later in Dresden and London, Venetian artist Rosalba Carriera drew hundreds of pastel portraits. In France, Quentin de La Tour devoted his whole life to portraits in pastel: He was the most famous portrait painter in the eighteenth century. Jean-Baptiste-Simeon Chardin showed a pastel portrait of his wife at the Paris Exhibition in 1775, and it is considered one of the best paintings of that time. Less than a hundred years later, Impressionism emerged, and with it, one of the best draftsmen in all art: Edgar Degas. Using colored paper as a background for his pastel figures, Degas resolved edges, shapes, and gradations by means of sharp strokes. His exquisitely rendered pastels were truly a merging of painting and drawing, but Degas was foremost a draftsman and is reputed to have said "I was born to draw."

The pastel medium is unique in that it has the properties of both painting and drawing. The works by the above artists were executed in pastel, but should they be considered pastel drawings or pastel paintings? They are like paintings because the surface of the paper is entirely worked, which is similar to oil painting. And in the past, pastels were regarded as paintings. Today, museums tend to classify pastels as drawings.

Fig. 387. This pastel drawing was made by the artist Francesc Serra. It was done with a limited range of colors (only three) and is shown here actual size.

387

fundamentals
of artistic
drawing

basic rules

One evening my good friends Ana and Jorge came to dinner. After the meal we were talking as we often do about art, and Ana expressed regret about not being able to draw. "I've never drawn in my life. I don't even know how to hold a pencil." So I gave her a 2B pencil and a sketchbook.

"Come on, have a try," I said. "Draw that chair. I'm sure you can."

Ana seemed perplexed. "But how?" and she burst into laughter.

But Ana was able to draw. First she drew a square, which was the basic shape of the chair. "Good," I said. "Now draw a rectangle on top of the square; its measurements should be more or less the same as the projecting part, or the seat, of the chair. Easy, isn't it? This is the first step to take when drawing any model: You must calculate the general shapes and proportions of the object before you."

"Proportions?"

"Yes, take a look and you'll see that the dimensions of the seat and the legs of the chair are approximately three parts wide and four parts high. Once you have solved the problems of relative height and width, you'll have to go on to the next basic element of drawing: perspective."

"Perspective?" repeated Ana, who was now becoming very interested.

"Yes, perspective. Please stand up here, in front of the chair, and look straight ahead. Imagine that there is a straight horizontal line. Imagine as well a point in the horizon, where all parallel lines, perpendicular to the horizon, meet the vanishing point, as it's called. You are now going to draw the horizon line and the vanishing point. By the way, how tall are you, Ana?"

"Well, 1.80 meters (5 foot 9 inches) with shoes on."

"To calculate the placement of the horizon line, I take the height of the seat, which without the back is more or less 20 inches (50 cm) and multiply it by three and a half. So the horizon line, which is equal to your height, will appear approximately three and a half times higher than the chair seat."

Fig. 389. This is the chair that Ana drew.

Fig. 390. Determining the correct dimensions and proportions is the first problem that the artist must solve. In this case, you begin by drawing a three-dimensional box, or cube, which corresponds to the projecting plane of the chair's seat.

Fig. 391. The next step is to determine perspective and depth. You need to calculate the horizon line, the point of view, and the vanishing points. At this point, the chair will begin to take shape.

Fig. 392. When drawing the human body, it's helpful to use the canon system, which divides the body into eight equal units, each one the lenght of a man's head.

389

390

DIMENSIONS AND PROPORTIONS

391

PERSPECTIVE

HORIZON LINE

CANON FOR THE HUMAN BODY: 8 HEADS TALL

"And then?" asked Ana.
"You only need to draw in the vanishing point, and then draw lines from the vertices of the rectangle of the seat to that vanishing point. Then draw another rectangle behind the first one, fitting it into the lines you drew as if the first one were made of glass, and you'll get a cube, or rather a rectangular prism in perspective." (Fig. 391).
"All right, but the drawing doesn't look like a chair."
"It will. But first you must calculate the size of the back in relation to the seat. To do this, draw another rectangle and then some lines (whose sides have to meet at the vanishing point), these will become the crossbeams of the chair's seat. After this, you'll have the basic structure complete. (Fig. 393). Then draw the chair within this structure. This is relatively easy since now you know the dimensions, relative proportions, and how to draw the chair in perspective."

"Terrific!"
Ana was drawing clumsily, but she was drawing!
"What else?"
"At this point, we must think about what the French artist Camille Corot called *values*. Values are basically light and shade effects: the gradation of tonal areas, value contrasts, and spatial complexities that bring life to your drawing."
"But how do you go about drawing people?"
"Well, fortunately for us there is a system, or canon, which shows the ideal proportions of the human body. The system was devised by the artists of ancient Greece and revived by the masters of the Renaissance. According to the canon, a man's height is eight times his head (Fig. 392). But, Ana, I can't tell you all about this in half an hour!"
"So you'll have to come to dinner every weekend," said my wife laughing.
"Great!" cried Ana.

Fig. 393. As you continue to construct the chair, you need to determine its basic structure, which consists of basic geometric forms, such as the cube and the rectangle.

Fig. 395. The final step is to model the form of the chair by introducing light and shaded areas. In this way you develop the values, contrast, and linear direction of the drawing.

Fig. 394. Once you have established the general shapes that make up the chair, these can then be fitted inside a cube to establish spatial position.

BASIC STRUCTURE

CONSTRUCTION FRAME

LIGHT AND SHADE

the mental calculation of dimensions

"*Exercise your eyes and learn to see the true length and breadth of objects.*" So directed Leonardo da Vinci in his *Treatise on Painting,* where he was writing about "sight training, which is the main factor in drawing and painting." In practice, this main factor means the observation of the model prior to drawing it, in which you calculate the dimensions and proportions. These calculations are based on three methods of observation:

A. Comparing certain distances with others.
B. Looking for reference points to establish basic lines.
C. Drawing imaginary lines in order to determine the position of certain objects in relation to others.

We are going to study in a practical way the applications of these formulas for observation. Look at Fig. 398, where a still life of a green pitcher, an apple, a bottle of brandy, a coffee cup is our example. All objects are on the table and the background is a white wall; the lighting is daylight coming in from the side.

Do you have everything ready? Drawing board, paper, pencil? . . . At this point an experienced artist would normally look at the model for a short while (say five or ten minutes) trying to understand in his or her own way the shapes, values, and colors, and calculating dimensions at the same time, comparing distances, looking for reference points.

Imagine the artist thinking aloud: "the height of the cup is two-thirds of the total width including the handle (Figs. 396A, B). The apple is the same as a sphere (Fig. 397). The total height of the bottle measures the

Figs. 396, 397, 398. Calculating dimensions and proportions is primarily done by comparing. For example, you will need to determine that the height of this cup is equal to two-thirds of its total width, including the handle; or that the apple, which is essentially a sphere, is as high as it is wide.

same distance from the edge of the pitcher to the edge of the cup, disregarding the handle (Fig. 399). The center of the total width coincides with the left edge of the bottle (Fig. 400). The dimensions of the pitcher correspond to a square. If I imagine a line in the center of that square, I get the upper limit of the cup, whose height is practically the same as the apple (Fig. 402). The height of the pitcher is half the height of the bottle. Both the base of the bottle and the base of the cup are at the same level. The width of the bottle is just a bit narrower than that of the cup and the apple (Fig. 403)."

If these mental calculations had been done on paper, you would have a rough structure that is practically complete, and you would be ready to draw the model (Fig. 404). But in this case you have only carried out part of the drawing in your head. The resolution–the real drawing–comes later.

Fig. 399. The first step is to calculate the dimensions and the proportions of the subject.

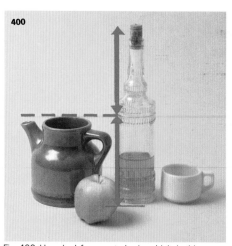

Fig. 400. Here, look for a central axis, which, in this case, coincides with the left side of the bottle.

Fig. 401. Establish reference points and imaginary lines. Here, it is determined that the jug is essentially a square shape; the upper edge of the cup coincides with the center of this square, and the height of the cup is almost the same as the height of the apple.

398

Fig. 402. In this example, you can see that the previous calculations have proven accurate. The cup does equal the lower half of the jug and the apple and the cup are the same height.

Fig. 403. Although some dimensions can't be exact, they can be adequate enough for the purposes of drawing by approximation.

Fig. 404. The sketch above is an example of how an artist uses a preliminary drawing to determine the general proportions of the subject. Without a sketch like this, it would be difficult for the artist to begin drawing.

calculating dimensions and proportions

What exactly are proportions? Obviously, there are variations. The head of a dwarf is larger in proportion to his body than that of the average person. But a classical statue from Hellenic Greece shows the ideal dimensions and proportions of the human form.

In drawing, *proportioning means representing the life-size figure or object on a smaller scale, keeping the relative measurements of the model proportional*. In the example shown here, the height of the cup approximates that of the apple; therefore, in your drawing, you will have to use the same scale of measurements so that these objects look in proportion to each other.

Of course, once you start to draw, the real dimensions of the model must be translated to the scale of the drawing paper. You will also need to consider the scale you want, so that the model does not appear too big or too small. To cope with changing scale, I recommend the use of two 90° angles cut out of black cardboard that you can put together to form a frame more or less rectangular or square in order to establish the best size for your scale. Remember, it is often a good idea to get closer to the model rather than farther away if you want to avoid a frame that minimizes the subject (Figs. 405 to 407).

The reduction of the model proportionally to the size of the paper is easily solved when you are copying from a picture or a photograph. You can do so by dividing the photograph or picture into a grid made up of squares, reducing or enlarging those squares on your paper. This systems has been used by artists throughout history, generally to enlarge sketches or transfer them onto wall or canvases. In the early sixteenth century, Albrecht Dürer wrote a treatise on dimensions and proportions in which he described and illustrated methods to solve this problem. One of these methods involved using a clear, squared-off piece of framed glass that was placed between him and the model. He then composed his picture by looking a what parts of the figure were enclosed in the various squares (Fig. 408). This idea was probably more theoretical than practical; as far as I know, nobody uses this system today. However, many artists use a grid system on paper to determine and compare dimensions. The most common method by which to determine basic proportions is the simple one that uses a pencil (or ruler or brush) placed in a vertical position and raised to the height of your eyes. You then hold out your arm and

405

Fig. 405. One way to understand better the significance of proportion, or ideal proportion, is to search out obvious disproportions, such as this carnival mask, which dwarfs the body upon which it rests.

407

Figs. 406, 407, 408. To decide how to frame the subject and determine how close the viewer should be to the objects in the drawing, take a cardboard frame painted black and study your

subject *before* beginning to paint. Better yet, do a quick postcard-size sketch suggesting the framing and composition of the subject.

Fig. 409. This is a drawing by Albrecht Dürer that he used to illustrate a treatise he wrote on dimensions and proportions. It shows a method for rendering a subject through a grid.

40

411

lace the pencil in front of the model and iterally measure the model against the pencil. To do this, you move your thumb up and down along the pencil until the part above the thumb coincides with the part of the model measured. Then repeat the same process, this time horizontally, comparing the dimensions (see Figs. 410 to 413). This process takes some time and experience, so for many artists this method can become a barrier that prevents them from proceeding with confidence. The proportions may be off somehow, draw carefully, continually comparing distances and using reference points, this barrier vanishes because eventually your mind will think proportionally and the correct dimensions will appear almost instinctively.

10

412

Figs. 410 to 413. The model's basic proportions are determined by measuring and comparing its height with its width. The measurements are taken facing the model, arm extended holding a pencil or brush in your hand. Then the relationship between the two measurements is calculated–for example, they may both be the same, or one may double the other.

413

fundamentals of perspective

Perspective is a complex system of drawing built on specific principles that has been the subject of hundreds of books. Simply stated, perspective drawing is a way of reproducing the appearance of three-dimensional reality on a flat plane. Since this is a book for artists and not architects, we can assume that we are primarily drawing from the natural world with the model in front of us. For artists, the essentials of perspective may be summed up with the following:

First basic principle:

THE HORIZON LINE

Except in special cases where you are drawing specific objects, such as a flower, an animal, or a hand, the horizon line is typically present in all subjects. As for its correct location, it is certainly not on the top of a mountain or at the bottom of a deep valley.

> The horizon line is always in front of you, at eye level.

A perfect example of this can be found in a seascape. If you look straight ahead, without raising or lowering your head, the horizon is the line formed by the edge of the water and the sky, which is, of course, at the height of your eyes. This applies if you are standing or sitting. If you crouch down–always looking ahead, of course–the horizon line comes down with you. If you climb to the top of a mountain, the horizon line goes up with you.

Second basic principle:

THE VIEWPOINT

The viewpoint is located on the horizon line, at the center of the viewer's field of vision–that is, right in front of you.

415

41

Third basic principle:

THE VANISHING POINT

The vanishing point is the place where receding parallel lines appear to converge. Vanishing points are always located on the horizon line. Locating vanishing points on that line gives the impression of depth or a third dimension.

The following are the three classes of perspective drawing:

1. *Parallel, or vanishing point, perspective.*
2. *Angular perspective, or perspective with two vanishing points.*
3. *Oblique perspective, or perspective with three vanishing points.*

On the next several pages, all three perspective systems will be explored on a practical level.

Fig. 414. A perspective drawing creates the illusion of reality by relating the observer, the object, and the picture plane. The horizon is assumed to be an infinite distance from the observer; the horizon line is placed at eye level.

Fig. 415. Since the height of the viewer's eye determines the location of the horizon line, it will change as the viewer's position changes. Thus, as shown here, the horizon line will drop if you assume a sitting position.

Fig. 416. If you look at a scene from a high point, the horizon line will also be high as you observe the view from this vantage point.

parallel perspective (one vanishing point)

The cube is the basic form in perspective because it can be used as a unit to measure height, width, and depth at the same time. Theoretically, the cube can be multiplied and divided into any combination of height, width, and depth to provide a basis for drawing any object. Consequently, in each case I will begin the lesson by explaining the process of drawing a cube in perspective. In this first case (the cube in parallel perspective), I have drawn the cube over the horizon line, although it could also be the other way around. Notice that in Fig. 417 the vanishing point is also the viewpoint.

421

I begin by drawing a square. Next, I draw four vanishing lines from the vertices of the square to the vanishing point (Fig. 418). Then, I draw horizontal line A, thus establishing the lower side of the cube by sight (Fig. 419). Finally, starting from horizontal line A, I draw the vertical B, completing the cube. But I still have to draw lines C and D as if the cube were transparent, in order to test its proportions. Now look at the photograph of Park Avenue in New York City (Fig. 421). It's a typical example of parallel perspective with one vanishing point which is, at the very same time, the point of view. Note the position of the viewer's eyes (just suppose you were there), and pay attention to the hundreds of windows, doors, and other openings, which vanish in order toward one point on the horizon to form third dimension. The impression of space is even more

evident here because of the contrast between the color of the foreground and the background; the blue gray gives the impression of depth.

Fig. 421. This photograph of Park Avenue in New York City is a good example of parallel perspective with a single vanishing point. Note the convergence of all parallel lines perpendicular to the horizon. The cubes added to this drawing give you a better understanding of this kind of parallel perspective.

angular perspective (two vanishing points)

422

423

424

For this exercise, I place the viewpoint more or less in the center of the cube and draw freehand the vertical corresponding to the closest edge. I place the vanishing points 1 and 2, and trace the first vanishing lines toward the right and toward the left (Fig. 422). I draw by eye the two lateral sides of the cube (Fig. 423), and then finish the drawing with the upper side. Notice that the angle formed by the base of the cube should always be more than 90º (Fig. 424).

The house in the photograph is an example of angular perspective with the vanishing points out of the drawing, which is usually what happens in practice. Observe the situation and perspective of the cubes in order to better understand the perspective of the house. In this example, though, there is an element that makes it a bit more difficult, by which I mean the roofs, whose edges meet at a special vanishing point, which, from the artistic point of view, is not essential. This is understandable since the inclination of the roofs can be drawn by eye, only taking into account the convergence–slightly visible–of the more slanted and visible lines such as B and C.

Fig. 425. Here we have a classic example of oblique perspective with two vanishing points that converge outside the image. Note the parallelism of the oblique lines going to the horizon on both sides. In this case, there is the exception of the inclined lines of the roofs, which can be resolved with a vanishing point that travels upward; but since we are drawing and not moking architectural renderings these lines can be drawn easily by sight.

425

oblique perspective (three vanishing points)

VANISHING POINT No. 1

PF1   HORIZON LINE   PF2

A   B

TO VANISHING POINT No. 3

426

TO VANISHING POINT No. 2

TO VANISHING POINT No. 2

90°

VANISHING POINT No. 3

If you look at a house or a building from above, you will see that neither the vertical or horizontal shapes are parallel. They all join at their vanishing points, with the peculiarity that two of these vanishing points are placed, as usual, on the horizon line; but the third one, corresponding to the vertical lines, is placed below that line. Of course, if you are standing at the base of a skyscraper, looking up, the vertical lines will vanish upward, toward that third vanishing point, which in this case will be above the horizon line. You can see this form of perspective applied to the images on these pages. Remember that the base angle AB should never be less than 90°.

Fig. 427. This is an example of an unusual kind of perspective, known as aerial perspective, which is especially useful for illustrations seen from above. There are three vanishing points, two that are oblique lines directed to vanishing points 1 and 2. There is also a third series of parallel lines that go to the vanishing point 3, which in this case is below the picture.

mosaics in perspective

428

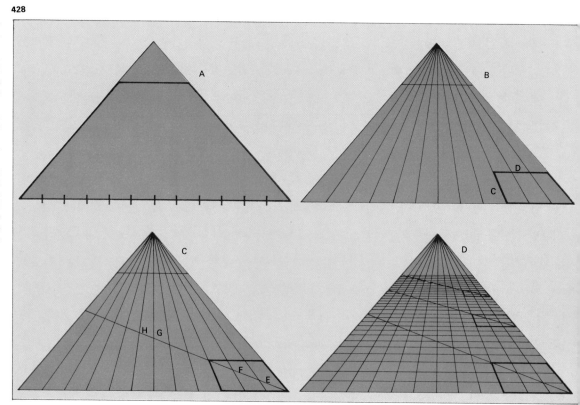

Fig. 428. **Process for drawing a mosaic in parallel perspective:**
A. Draw in perspective the total perimeter of the mosaic, and then, on the ground line, mark the number of tiles that make up the mosaic vertically.
B. Taking three lines of tiles, draw by eye a square such as C.D.
C. Trace a diagonal that crosses the points E, F, G, H.
D. Crossing this diagonal with the vertical parallels gives you the points of reference to trace the corresponding horizontal lines, which will complete the mosaic. Following the same process, you can repeat the sequence to infinity.

429

Fig. 429. **How to draw a mosaic in oblique perspective:**

A. Draw the *line of measurements* next to the lower vertex of the plane; divide this line into equal spaces (*a, b, c, d*); and trace the line A, from vertex to vertex, to establish the vanishing point for the diagonals.
LINE OF MEASUREMENTS

B. From points *a, b, c, d* trace vanishing lines to the left point to obtain points *e, f, g, h.*

C. Using these last points *e, f, g, h* draw the vanishing lines to the right point.

D. Now, trace line *B* from the vanishing point of the diagonals to the vertex of the *C.* tile. This way you can draw three more vanishing lines to the left.

E) The latter lines will now let you draw three more lines to the point at the right

F) Continue in the same fashion until the whole perspective area is covered.

dividing spaces in depth

Fig. 430, A and B. This building, seen from the front, is a symmetrical construction. You can draw this building in perspective by dividing its basic rectangle into two or more spaces with X-shaped lines. Using this method, you will automatically find the center of each space.

Fig. 431. This illustration of an old Roman-style church was an exercise in perspective. The repeated receding spaces and geometrical scheme of the façade can be solved using perspective, as seen in Fig. 432 below.

430

A

B

431

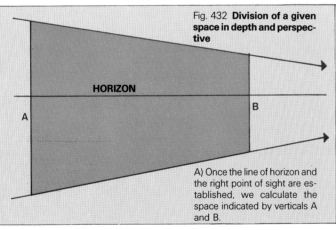

Fig. 432 **Division of a given space in depth and perspective**

HORIZON

A   B

A) Once the line of horizon and the right point of sight are established, we calculate the space indicated by verticals A and B.

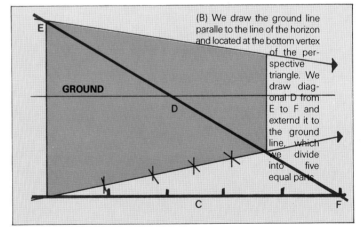

(B) We draw the ground line paralle to the line of the horizon and located at the bottom vertex of the perspective triangle. We draw diagonal D from E to F and externd it to the ground line, which we divide into five equal parts.

GROUND

E   D   F

C

(C) Now we draw diagonal lines from the divisions to point G and obtain the division of spaces in depth and perspective for a given distance.

G

432

shadows in perspective

Imagine the interior of a room seen in angular perspective, with some furniture or basic shapes, a lamp hanging from the center of the ceiling, and a human figure standing under the lamp. The horizon line is at the level of the eyes of the figure, and the vertices of the walls converge to the vanishing points. Vanishing point 1 is inside the room, and vanishing point 2, is outside the picture (Fig. 433). As soon as we switch on the light, the projected shadows appear (Fig. 434).

Let's see how these shadows are produced. The first factor to take into account is: *Artificial light is conveyed radially and in a straight line* (Fig. 434).

If we could materialize the beam of light that illuminates every shape, we could see a series of angles whose vertices are always at the source of light. Consequently,

The source of light becomes a vanishing point of light (VPL). This new vanishing point allows the projection of all the necessary angles toward all the planes, edges, and vertices, determining the shape of the shadow. But there is still an element missing: *The vanishing point of the shadow (VPS).* The placement of this point is given partly by a vertical line from the point of light to the floor, and partly by a simple calculation of perspective, projecting to the floor the placement of the light to the ceiling. *Sunlight is conveyed in parallel lines.*

Therefore, when images are seen in oblique perspective (from above), shadows do not have any perspective at all (Fig. 435). In normal perspective, with images against the light, you will have two vanishing points: *The vanishing point of light, which is the sun, and the vanishing point of shadows, placed on the horizon, under the sun.* Finally, if you are working with a frontal light or with a frontal-lateral light, you will also have to work with two vanishing points: *the vanishing point of shadows, on the horizon, under the sun, and the vanishing point of light, placed under the vanishing point of shadows.* Always consider the incidence of the angle of illumination on the model (Fig. 437).

guidelines

When we draw in oblique perspective, which is the perspective system most frequently used, it often happens that one vanishing point and sometimes even two disappear out of the picture. Such is the case with the house shown on page 118 (Fig. 425) and in the drawings shown here. In this case it is very difficult to establish the right perspective for all the elements in the model. Studying and practicing the exercises in perspective explained on the preceding pages will help you understand how to use guidelines for establishing the correct perspective in your drawings. The sketches at bottom illustrate the steps to building up these guidelines.

438

439

Fig. 438. When drawing in perspective subjects such as this one, where the vanishing points disappear outside the picture, you will probably be able to place the convergence of the lines by sight. But it is good to know that there is a formula you can use.

Fig. 439. A. You fit the model starting from the nearest vertical (a), and trace the lines b and c, which limit, from above and from below, the total form of the model in perspective.

B. Now divide the nearest vertical (a) in a certain number of parts. Prolong the vanishing line approximately one cm out of the square and draw verticals d and e. Now divide the latter into the same number of parts vertical a is divided.

C. Finally draw lines to unite A with A, B with B and so on, until you get a guideline that will allow you to draw all the items in the model in perfect perspective.

perspective: examples

Drawing the circle in perspective

A	B	C	D	E
			WRONG	**RIGHT**

Fig. 440 A. To draw a circle in perspective, you first need to draw a square and divide it with diagonals to locate the center. Then draw perspective lines through the center to bisect the sides. Connect these points with a curved line, and you have a circle in perspective.

Fig. 440 B. The farther the circle is from the level of the horizon line, the more evident is its shape. Thus, a thin circular plate placed at the level of the horizon will be transformed into a line.

Fig. 440 C. As illustrated above, achieving the correct perspective of a cylinder requires a preliminary drawing to fit the shape into a square or rectangular prism.

Fig. 440 D, E. The above illustration (D) shows the three common mistakes that people make when drawing cylinders. Top: Where the side intersects the base, the lines are angular rather than curved. Center: The horizontal thickness is wider

than the vertical. Bottom: The upper circle of the cylinder is drawn with the same foreshortening as the lower circle; the lower circle should be less elliptical.

441

442

Figs. 441, 442, 443. Here are three examples of parallel perspective with a single vanishing point and the lines of the horizon placed at different levels. This explains why the house in Fig. 442 offers a typical eye-level perspective; the country house (Fig. 441) appears somewhat small, as it is seen from above ground level; and the church, seen from below, gives a sort of monumental impression.

443

444

OBLIQUE PERSPECTIVE

Figs. 444 and 445. These are two examples of oblique perspective with two vanishing points and the line of the horizon at eye-level. Both have a similar viewpoint.

445

PF1

PF2

Figs. 446 and 447. This drawing indicates how to calculate the perspective center by using the X-shaped cross method. On the right is an example of spatial depth.

447

446

cézanne's formula

Shortly before he died, Paul Cézanne wrote a series of letters to the painter Emile Bernard, who was a passionate admirer of Cézanne's art. They had met two years before, in 1904, and Cézanne became Bernard's tutor. They painted together for a while and later corresponded with each other. This series of letters is an important written proof of Cézanne's methods and theories, the most famous of which states that the basic shapes can be seen in every item of nature. On the 15th of April, 1904, Cézanne told Bernard:

Let me say again what I have already told you: Deal with nature through cubes, spheres and cylinders, everything in the right perspective.

This idea had already been observed by Rubens when he wrote, "The basic structure of the human figure can be reduced to cubes, circles, and triangles." But Cézanne took this concept further to include all form, rather than just

448

Fig. 448. Paul Cézanne. *Self-portrait*. Pencil. Art Institute of Chicago. Cézanne said that in nature, everything is modeled according to three fundamental forms: the cube, the cylinder, and the sphere.

the human figure. His ideas had a profound impact on Matisse, Braque, and Picasso, and contributed to the birth of Cubism.

If you analyze the structure of objects near you, or if you look at a house, a car, or a flower pot, for example, you will notice that they are composed of one of the basic geometric figures. Thus, if you are able to draw a sphere, a cube, or a cylinder, you should be able to draw everything.

On page 100, under the heading "Wash techniques in practice," you were asked to build a cylinder, a cube, a pyramid, and a rectangular prism. For this exercise, you need a sphere, which could be a small white ball (if the ball is of a different color you can paint it with white spray paint). Try drawing these shapes from the models, in various sizes and positions, in parallel and oblique perspective, and seen from different angles. This is a very useful first step, from which you can progress to more advanced aspects of drawing.

449

450

Figs. 449 and 450. In general, any object in the world can be drawn, as Cézanne said, by beginning with basic geometric forms such as the cube, a rectangle, a cylinder, a pyramid, a cone, or a sphere.

boxing up, structure, sketch

How do we begin a drawing? Some people begin a drawing with one of the two basic forms of perspective; many draw a square or a rectangle or a sketch of the model. But only a few go straight to the specific, individual shapes. However, they all must consider the relation of the height of a model to its width and the problem of dimensions and proportions. They must draw or at least imagine a *box*, a square or a rectangle, a cube or a prism, where they can introduce the model. In other words, *boxing-up* the image is the first thing we do when drawing. We shall distinguish first between two groups of subjects or models:

1. *Models whose structure may be reduced to one basic three-dimensional shape.*
2. *Models whose structure may only be reduced to flat geometric shapes.*

In the first group, we should include all the bodies whose shape is given by a cube or its derivatives such as prisms, cylinders, cones, pyramids, or spheres. As for the second group, we should include in it all the objects that do not share the above-mentioned feature, such as the human figure, animals, plants, flowers.

The cube

Learning to draw a cube in the right perspective will help you draw many different objects, from a piece of furniture to a skyscraper. Look at the example on the following page, which shows the drawing of a church carried out step by step, using a cube as the basis for the drawing.

Fig. 454. I start by drawing the two verticals (A and B), corresponding to the two parallel lines that define the tower of the church. Previously, I have calculated the proportional length or height of both lines, as well as the distance between them. I now draw in the horizon line; then, I calculate and draw by eye the inclination of the oblique lines that go to the vanishing points 1 and 2. The latter is outside of the drawing paper's edge, so I draw the vertical C. I divide both C and A into equal parts and then I build a guide-pattern–always by eye–according to the way it was done on page 123.

Fig. 455. I calculate the dimensions and proportions of the two parts of the church. I compare width and height, and I draw the structure of the model in perspective.

Fig. 451. Some artists begin with perspective lines to draw a basic form of the model.

Fig. 452. Other artists start a work by drawing a square, a rectangle, or a sketch of the subject's outline.

Fig. 453. A few artists venture to begin a drawing by drawing in the specific contours of the model, which states the shape in fine detail.

Fig. 456. I begin the actual drawing of the church filling in the shadows at the same time. The guide-pattern helps me now to locate in perspective the rooftop of the steeple and the side windows. Notice how the calculation of the perspective center has been made, in order to place the church's cross, and the top (or vertex) of the roof.

Figs. 457 and 458. There is only one question left: the distribution in perspective of the windows along the side of the lower building, which could be solved by dividing the spaces in depth (see page 121). However, I have calculated this by eye with the help of the reference given by the actual model. The rest is a matter of adjusting light and shade, drawing in complementary elements such as trees or hills.

The glass cube

Whenever you draw a basic shape in perspective, particularly a cube or a rectangular prism, it is best to draw the interior lines of the structure, as if it were made of glass. This will allow you to control proportions and structure errors, such as the ones you can see in cube A, made evident by the glass cube B. Cube A is not really a cube but a prism. This is made evident by the interior side C, which is completely out of proportion. The convergence of some vanishing lines is incorrect. The vertical D does not coincide with the vertex of the angle E, and so on.

454

A

D

B

C

VP 1

VP 2

HORIZON LINE

455

456

457

458

boxing up, structure, sketch

Flat geometrical box

The model is now a German shepherd (Fig. 460A). We have no basic cube or perspective here. However, every model, no matter how complex, can be boxed up within a square or rectangle. We must calculate the full height of the model in relation to its width. Frequently you will find that the main body of a particular subject has other accessory shapes that extend out of this main body (Fig. 460B). If such is the case, the boxing up should enclose the main body and should omit the accessory shapes (Fig. 460C).

Tight box and countermold

The next step demonstrates the transition from the flat geometrical square or rectangle to a tighter type of box (Fig. 460D), by drawing a structure closely related to the shape of the model. Draw it in a rough way, disregarding small details. The drawing will be a set of curved and broken lines. Be aware of the "negative space" (Fig. 460E). Try to see definite shapes, which act as a sort of mold to help adjust the shape of the model.

Boxing up with shadows

The edges of shadows are also a good reference as boxing-up lines, especially for models with sharp contrasts. Light and shade effects are often essential elements in a drawing. It is important to learn to draw areas of light and shade, disregarding small details, and to know how to modify or intensify the shadows.

When boxing up with lead pencil, use a soft pencil and be sure your strokes are very light so that you can modify them with an eraser. Use paper that is good enough to withstand moderate erasure and enable redrawing on the sketch, because it requires a great deal of practice to get the rendering exactly as you want it on the first try.

Boxing up requires drawing with slight, steady strokes and drawing quickly but carefully. It means keeping in mind dimensions and proportions, constantly comparing distances, finding reference points, and imagining lines to locate levels, contours, and shapes. "Boxing up means keeping an eye on everything," Ingres told his pupils, "so that the drawing can be shown at any moment with the final character which will grow more and more refined."

Figs. 459. Sometimes, within the initial fitting process, there are subjects where the box or total structure of a subject (A) can be reduced and limited to the major masses, eliminating the secondary shapes (B).

Fig. 460. **Visual process of fitting in a geometric or flat box.** The model **A B**. I start the sketch with a rectangular box, which exactly fits the height and width of the model. Then, inside this box **C**, I draw a scheme of the dog's outline, taking as points of reference: the nose, which is placed at a third of the height of the box (*a*); the point of the right ear and the tip of the tongue (imaginary line *b*); the point *c*, which goes to the vertex of the angle formed by the ear and the top of the head (*d*). **D**. Imagine an inclined line *a-d*, where I draw the profile of the nose; then, another horizontal line under the nose, together with shape *e*, will allow me to draw the profile of the upper jowl. Now I draw the eye, checking that it is placed in the center of the rectangular box. Then, I trace lines *f* and *g*, which correspond to the profile of the right ear and the forehead. I finish drawing the other eye and the black spot on the nose. **E**. Now, it is time to check, by studying the *negative space h* of the drawing. In them, we should see definite shapes which act as a countermold of the outline. **F**. Draw in the lines that limit the dark and medium-value areas, for they are also a valuable reference to constructing the drawing. **G**. General checking of proportions and dimensions, by erasing if necessary, finally, by resolving values. **H** and **I**. Assessment of the correct amount of contrast.

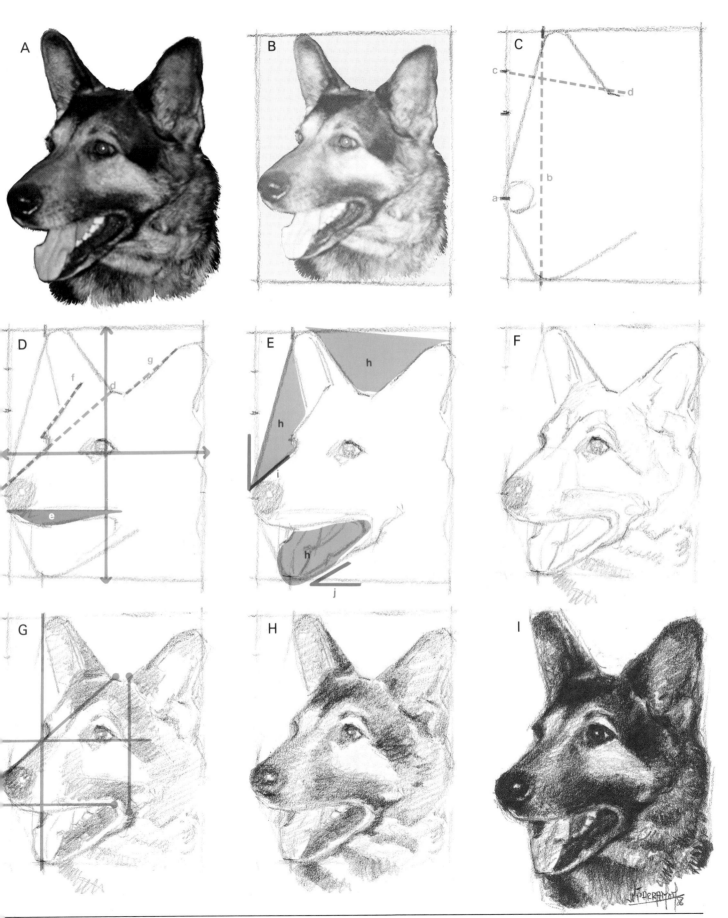

light and shadow

The art historian Heinrich Wolfflin, after comparing drawings and paintings by Dürer, Aldegrever, and Bronzino with works by Rembrandt, Van Dyck, and Velázquez, stated that in the Baroque period the art of drawing changed in style. It stopped being the art of lines and contours, and became a pictorial art where we see the mass instead of just the lines, and where we ignore contours, and appreciate the beauty of the model and the meaning of the picture through dark and light. In other words, this means that if you are drawing with tones, values, grisailles and gradations you are, in effect, "painting." This is the basic principle behind the concept of "drawing-painting." There are three main factors that allow the artist to express his ideas through light:

> *The direction of the light*
> *The amount of light*
> *The quality of the light*

The five most commonly used directions of light, which apply equally to drawing and painting, are:

1. *Front light* illuminates the model from the front, casting virtually no shadow. It is not very appropriate for learning how to draw; without the effects of light and shade the model lacks definition and volume (Fig. 461).
2. *Front-lateral light* falls on the subject at an angle of 45º. This is the direction that best explains shapes and volumes (Fig. 462).
3. *Lateral light* falls from one side, throwing the other side into shadow, which dramatizes the subject. It is used for general figure studies and sometimes in portraits as well (Fig. 463).
4. *Back-light or semi-back-light* comes from behind and throws the planes the artists sees into deep shadow. It is frequently used in modern figurative painting (Fig. 464).
5. *Top light* comes from a lamp above or a window high up on a wall. This direction is ideal for drawing and painting. It is a classical type of illumination (Fig. 465).

Besides the above kinds of lighting, you can also light a subject from below. Goya used this lighting for his work, *The Shootings on the 3rd of May.*

The second factor, *the amount of light*, has a great influence on contrast. A model illuminat-

Figs. 461 to 465. Commonly used directions of light: Below frontal light; second row, from left to right, frontal light, lateral light, back lighting, and top lighting.

461

462

463

464

465

466

Figs. 466, 467. The quality of the light influences the values and contrast found on the model. On the left, a model lit by a direct light from artificial light; on the right, the same image, under a diffused natural light, offers less contrast and definition.

ed with a weak light, such as a 25-watt bulb or a candle, casts very dark shadows, almost black. On the other hand, very powerful lighting, particularly if it is diffuse, diminishes the intensity of shadows and contrast.

The quality of light is determined by its type and placement of the light source and is closely related to the quantity. There are two types to consider:

1. *Direct light* from a bulb or the sun illuminates the model. Shadows appear precise and create sharp contrasts. (Fig. 466).
2. *Diffused light* is the type of light seen on a cloudy day. It is also the type of light that reaches the model through a door or a window—including the above-mentioned top light. It produces soft shadows with blurred edges (Fig. 467).

Finally, we must consider the factors that condition the effects of light and shade:

1. *Light*: Illuminated areas where the color seen is that of the model itself.
2. *Brightness*: Effect that is achieved by means of contrast. Remember that a white may appear whiter depending on how dark the surrounding tone is.
3. *Shade*: This is the part of the model that does not receive any light directly. We can distinguish there chiaroscuro, or lights and darks, and the reflected light.
4. *Reflected light*: This is the result of light on the shaded parts of the model. It always appears whenever there is a light-colored object opposite the light, which may be a good solution in some cases.
5. *Joroba*: This Spanish word meaning the darkest part of shadows, between the reflection and the illuminated part.
6. *Bright-dark*: It is the area between the illuminated part and the shaded areas. It means the same as *chiaroscuro*.
7. *Cast shadow*: This is the shadow cast by the model.

Fig. 468. Example of the effects of light and shade in a lead pencil drawing of a plaster cast. This drawing is a copy of *The Slave* by Michelangelo.

value

Value, either in drawing or painting, refers to the degree of darkness or lightness we see on the model. Values are the same as tones. Thanks to values, we can suggest volume and depth in our drawing.

Value is a way of comparing. Its use implies the mental classification of tones and shades in order to render properly the darker, the lighter, and the intermediate. Here are a few rules to make this comparison easier:

1. *Observe the nature of light*: In real life, the shape of bodies is not determined by outlines. Bodies are not linear, as if they were made of wire. The shape of things is conveyed by a continuum of surfaces modeled by light.
In order to render the pictorial drawing the historian Wöfflin speaks of, we could begin a drawing directly with various shades of gray. This would create a lineless drawing in which limits and contours are defined by tones as you can see in the drawing at right (Fig. 469). Notice the highlighted area from the chest and the hip down to the knees. Its configuration is described by a light tone in the background which defines the shape of the figure without lines.

469

470 **471** **472**

Fig. 469 (opposite). A wide range of values, from an intense black to a light gray, enables the artist to suggest the volume of objects, which are never seen as line but as a composition of surfaces modeled by light.

Figs. 470, 471, 472. Note in this step-by-step study the process of building up values in a pencil drawing. Also note how all areas of the figure are worked on simultaneously and progressively.

2. *Use values progressively*: This is the next step after boxing up when you need to fill in the specific model's shape and lighting. But both factors have to be dealt with simultaneously and progressively, rather than stopping to finish completely this or that area.

It is a matter of studying and placing values correctly step by step: starting with a light range of grays (Fig. 470), proceeding to more intense tones (Fig. 471), progressing to dark grays and blacks within as wide a range as possible (Fig. 472).

3. *Squint to study an object.* Squinting enables you to see values more clearly. Objects become more defined and contrast is exaggerated, all of which makes the comparative values much easier to see.

the direction of strokes

In the chapter on light and shade in his book, *Treatise on Painting*, Leonardo da Vinci wrote, "Compare the direction of lines; take into consideration which lines go in which direction and where they are stronger or more evident." Pencil strokes in drawing, or brushstrokes in painting, can be vertical, horizontal, slanted, wavy, or circular. Many artists of the past and present draw or paint following a "logical" direction in their strokes, following the shape, structure, and texture of the model. Slanted strokes are the most widely used, particularly for quick sketches. Horizontal strokes might be used for the sea and sky, circular for the clouds, slanted or circular for the basic cylindrical shapes of the human body.

However, there are remarkable exceptions to these directions of strokes. In many of his pastel drawings, in particular the female nudes, Edgar Degas solved the whole drawing background, figure and minor details using only vertical strokes. Sometimes this direction is also used for landscapes. There is, however, a general rule which can be summarized as follows:

The direction of the stroke should follow or explain the form whenever possible.

Fig. 473. These two drawings illustrate how the direction of the line or the brushstroke is conditioned by the texture of the model. In the human body, the direction of the line can be diagonal, vertical, or horizontal strokes, but in general they follow the cylindrical shape of the body. In the example of the drawing of a child's head, it is logical that the strokes follow the general contours of the hair.

473

474

Fig. 474. The general rule to "envelop the form" with the direction of the line has a few exceptions, such as this one where most lines of the landscape are vertical.

contrast

When we compare two or more tones or values in a drawing, we are seeing a new effect: contrast. It can be soft, if it is based on tones of similar intensity, whether they are all bright or all dark. Contrast can be sharp, with a prevalence of light tones versus dark tones and hardly any intermediate tones. But a drawing can also contain a wide range of tones, deep black, dark gray, medium gray and so on, up to pure white.

Contrast, together with values and the direction of light, is a valuable method or artistic expression. In his work *The System of the Arts*, the philosopher Friedrich Hegel wrote: "The character of objects depends mainly on the way they are illuminated. The theme of a picture is deeply related to the way it is illuminated."

Now, moving on to practical examples: a child's face will express his age, complexion, and character much better in a drawing with soft contrast. Ingres advised his pupils: "Women's portraits must not be very dark. They should be as light as possible."

Fig. 475. The law of simultaneous contrast states that *white will look even whiter the darker the tone that surrounds it. And gray will be more intense the lighter the tone that surrounds it.* For example, the shaded areas in figure A appear to be a more intense gray on a white background than the shaded areas in figure B. The black background gives us the optical illusion of a lighter gray, because of the law of simultaneous contrast.

The contrast of tones provides us with some physiological phenomena very important for the artist's work. One of them, *law of simultaneous contrasts*, can be expressed in this way:

1. *White looks whiter as the dark tone surrounding it is increased in depth.*
2. *A gray tone appears more intense as the light tone surrounding it is lightened.*

You can check this optical effect right now. Place in front of you a sheet of white paper and a sheet of black paper. Put in the center on the black sheet a small square of white paper, about one and a half inches square. You will see that the white of the small square appears whiter than the white sheet of paper because of the effect of simultaneous contrast. If you draw a gray shape on a white background, the latter will look lighter than the former.

From a practical point of view, the law of simultaneous contrasts means that in order to draw the brightness of a glass or the glitter of a metallic object, the shimmer of light on the sea, or any glossy surface, it is necessary to darken the surrounding tones. It also means that by darkening a tone which is juxtaposed with another, the latter becomes lighter, and a stronger contrast between these two tones is achieved.

Artists often use the white of the paper to enhance the effect of a shimmer or a gleam. They may render the white surfaces and shapes of the model, such as the white of a dress or a snowy landscape with an off-white or light gray. It is worth remembering this theory:

No object is absolutely white.

The poet, philosopher, painter, and playwright Leon Battista Alberti wrote in 1436: "Remember that you should never paint a surface so white that it cannot be made much whiter. The painter does not have a white much whiter to reproduce the brightness of a sword. Thus, even if you are painting snow-white clothes, stop before you reach the whitest tone."

475

contrast and atmosphere

Imagine you are going to draw a still life. You choose your model, determine the composition, study the illumination but . . . be careful! This moment is particularly important. You can create a deeper or a softer contrast depending on the direction, amount, and quality of light. You can illuminate the background or leave it dark. You can take into consideration Leonardo's advice, "The background should be dark where the subject is illuminated and should be light where the subject is in shadow." Then, when you are already drawing or painting, you can darken or lighten certain areas and spots creating contrasts to explain shapes more clearly. Velázquez, El Greco, Delacroix, Cézanne, and many other great masters invented contrasts to enhance shapes.

Atmosphere

Atmosphere means air and space and suggests the third dimension: depth. Between the place you are sitting and the nearest wall there is space, and in this space there is atmosphere. We must be aware of this atmosphere to simulate it in our drawings, although it does not convey itself to us clearly or palpably.
As a typical example of atmosphere, see the adjoining drawing made early in the morning

at the fishermen's wharf in Barcelona (Fig. 478). The day was a bit cloudy and the sun was not completely high in the sky yet, so there was a sort of mist acting as a veil between the shapes and the viewer. This helps gauge the distance between one object and another. There is an old boat and another one half-sunk, outlined in bright, humid colors, emphasizing the contrast between light and dark. The clear water moves there with glassy reflections and a metallic sheen. Further away, there is a group of three or four boats whose shapes are less visible, as if we were looking through colored glass. There are no definite outlines or sharp contrasts here. Finally, blurred in the distance, we see the mist, the atmosphere, some tints whose silhouettes barely hint at a ship, and some buildings and smoke stacks.
This example helps to summarize the factors governing the sensation of atmosphere:

1. *Bright contrast occurs in close objects and decreases as the distance increases.*
2. *Colors fade and become grayer as the distance increases.*
3. *Marked brilliance occurs at the nearest points in contrast to those farther away.*

To quote again from Hegel's *System of the Arts*, where he relates the concepts of atmosphere

Fig. 476. In accordance with Leonardo da Vinci: "The background surrounding a figure should offer darkness where the area is illuminated and lightness where the area is shaded." This observation is evident in Gustave Courbet's portrait of Théophile Gautier. Here, Courbet darkens the background near the highlighted area of the face, but lightens the background tone adjacent to the dark hair.

Fig. 477. Vincent Van Gogh, *Study of Trees.* Charcoal pencil and white chalk on paper. Kroeller-Mueller Museum. The subject of this drawing is the arabesque created by the shape of the trunks and branches of the trees. Van Gogh drew this scene with intense grays and blacks on a light, almost white background, an effect which creates extraordinary contrast.

and contrast, "People usually think that the foreground is the lightest and the background is the darkest. But the truth is that the foreground is the darkest and, at the same time, the brightest. That is, the contrast of light and shade in the foreground is more intense, and at the same time, the outlines become more definite. The more distant objects are, the lighter and grayer their color is and the less determined their shadows are because the opposition of light and shade gradually disappears." But what are we supposed to do when all the objects are in the foreground? How should we draw the atmosphere in a still life, a portrait, or a group of figures? All those models are three-dimensional, so we need to represent the space between them. Of course, the atmosphere is not visible, as in a misty landscape. But we have another option: blending the outline of the farthest objects, even if their relative distance is very small. Remember that when we look at an object less than two yards away we spontaneously focus on that point and blur the rest of objects in front of and behind it, just as a camera does. In a still life we will draw the objects in the foreground more precisely, and the ones in the background less precisely. Objects are alive since they have color and reflect the light, and light vibrates. On the other hand our vision is not entirely steady. These factors indicate that, in a sense, a good drawing is somewhat ethereal. Even when drawing a portrait, we often stress almost intuitively the sharpness of the eyes, and we tend to soften our line when we draw the contour of the head or the ear, in an attempt to create the sensation that the head is not flat. In other words, we create the illusion of depth.

478

Fig. 478. This scene of a harbor is an example of using dark-light contrast in the foreground area, and color in the background area.

Fig. 479. As seen in this portrait, when the model is observed close up, the perception of depth can be suggested by "putting out of focus," or rendering very softly those areas that are farthest away.

Fig. 480. In a portrait the suggestion of atmosphere or depth is enhanced by juxtaposing highly resolved, detailed areas against softly rendered, diffused areas.

479

480

the human figure

481

Fig. 481. This is a scene from a life drawing class at the School of Fine Arts of Barcelona. The classroom had about thirty students and two models. The students' area was lit by fluorescent lighting and the models were lit by a powerful floodlight which gave a backlighting effect.

Fine Arts School, Barcelona. Life drawing class. The classroom is quite large. There are more than thirty pupils drawing, more girls than boys, and two or three adults. There are two models: Near one of the walls, on a platform, there is a naked man proportioned according to Velazquez's models in *Vulcan's Forge,* on the other side of the room, there is a woman as young as Renoir's bathers. It is daylight, but the curtains are closed, and the students work by artificial light, fluorescent light for the students and tungsten floodlights for the models. Everyone is paying great attention. The only sound that can be heard is that of the charcoal against the paper. The atmosphere is so in-

tense, there is almost a spiritual feeling in the room.

In all cities all over the world, in public or private schools, in societies or academies, there are classes in life drawing. There are professional models who go to an artist's studio to pose for a few hours. Studying and practicing from nature is essential. The human figure is an ideal model.

About the middle of the last century, there was a painter in Paris named Troyon. He was a master of drawing *en plein air,* or outdoors. The young Impressionists used to visit him and listen to his advice. Claude Monet, in a letter of May 19, 1859, to Eugène Boudin, an-

Fig. 482. Two sketches of a nude by the artist Badia Camps drawn with black and gray chalk. Note the position of the hips *contrapposto* of the standing model, where you can check the tilting of the pelvis, the back, and the shoulder blades, regulated by the spinal column. Note also in the sitting figure the accuracy of the lines used to suggest the features of the face, the hair, and the ear.

482

other artist, wrote: "I've been to visit Troyon. We talked about the best way to learn to draw, and he told me that in order to learn to draw, one has to go to a studio where the only assignments are drawings from nature."

the canon of the human figure

There is a perfect formula, called a canon, for boxing up and proportioning the human figure, using the height of the head as the basic measurement. The first canon was established by the ancient Greek sculptor Polyclitus in the fifth century B.C. The basic measurement used by Polyclitus was the width of a hand, which was later transformed during the Renaissance into the height of the head. Polyclitus's canon was equivalent to seven and a half heads.

483

Women are proportionally shorter than men.

The module is given by the heighy of the head.

The nipples are lower than a man's.

The navel is located lower.

The pubis is in the center.

In profile buttocks prolude beyond the line of cald and shoulder-blade

During the Renaissance, this canon was studied by several artists, including Leonardo and Dürer. However, though some artists held that Polyclitus was right, others established canons of eight or eight and a half heads. Leonardo insisted it had to be ten. Eventually, by the beginning of this century, it was determined that:

The canon for the ideal figure is eight heads high by two heads wide.

This refers to *ideal height.* The *normal height* of a figure is as Polyclitus said, seven and a half heads, and the height of the so-called heroic figure, such as Moses, Tarzan, or Superman, is eight and a half heads. As far as I know, no artist draws figures to the canon or uses it systematically as if it were squared paper. But all good professionals know about it, and when it comes to drawing, either from life or the imagination you must remember these dimensions and proportions (Figs. 483, 484):

1. *The proportion of the body seen from the front is eight heads high and two heads wide.*
2. *The level of the shoulders is one third of the way down module nᵒ. 2.*
3. *The nipples are on the line of module nᵒ. 2.*
4. *The distance between the nipples is one module (one head).*
5. *The navel is a little below module nᵒ. 3.*
6. *The elbows are at waist-level.*
7. *The pubis is in the center of the body.*
8. *The knee is just above module nᵒ. 6.*
9. *The male figure in profile, the calf protrudes beyond the vertical line of the buttocks and shoulder blade.*

The female figure differs from the male at the following points:

1. *The female figure is shorter than the male by about 4 inches (10 cm).*
2. *The shoulders are proportionally narrower.*
3. *The breasts and nipples are slightly lower.*
4. *The waist is somewhat narrower.*
5. *The hips are proportionally broader.*
6. *In profile the buttocks protrude beyond the vertical line of the shoulder blade and the calf.*

Whenever you draw a figure from nature, remember these dimensions. Then there's no way you can be wrong.

484

The module is the same as the height of the head.

The nipples coincide with module no. 2

The navel is placed in module no. 3

The hand is the same as the height of the face.

The knee is above module 6.

Figure in profile. The calf of the log juts out of the vertical line formed by the buttocks and shoulder blades.

anatomy: structure of the human figure

Polyclitus and Praxiteles sculpted human figures just by observing the model and interpreting from nature, without being schooled in anatomy. But Michelangelo and all the Renaissance artists showed the necessity of a deeper knowledge in artistic anatomy. Ingres said, "To express the surfaces of the human body we must first know its structure."

Artistic anatomy has been the subject of many books and treatises, and is too large a topic to discuss here completely. Perhaps your interest in drawing will lead you to acquire a good book on artistic anatomy. However, we shall discuss here one very common pose in figure drawing, which is understood better when one has a knowledge of artistic anatomy.

Fig. 485. *A lesson in Anatomy.* Anonymous engraving, Louvre, Paris. Using perspective and anatomy as a basis for drawing began during the Renaissance. Both Leonardo and Michelangelo dissected corpses, which at the time was considered a sacrilege and was forbidden by law.

485

Figs. 486, 487. A knowledge of artistic anatomy is necessary in order to make good drawings of the human figure. To learn anatomy, you should study the bones, muscles, and tendons of the human body.

486

COLLARBONE
SHOULDERBLADE
RIBS
HUMERUS
SPINE
SACRUM-ILIAC
RADIUS
ULNA
FEMUR
PATELLA
TIBIA
FIBULA

487

STERNUM-CLEIDO-MASTOID
TRAPEZIUS
PECTORAL
SERRATED
BICEPS
PRONATOR
SUPINATOR
ABDUCENT
TOE EXTENSOR

DELTOID
TRICEPS
DORSAL
GLUTEUS
GEMELLUS
ACHILLES' TENDON

The contrapposto

When the model puts the weight of his or her body on one leg and at the same time relaxes the other, we have what was called, during the Renaissance, contrapposto. We shall define it as the hip position, though anthropologists prefer the term *ischiatic position*, because the *ischia* (the two lower edges of the pelvic bones), shifts from one side to the other when the body rests on one leg or on the other. This position also influences the chest and the collar bone, which shift to the other side, inclining the shoulders and twisting the spine (Figs. 488, B, and C). Notice now on the left profile in Fig. 489, the prominence of the iliac crest of the pelvis (a); the soft "valley" produced by the lack of bones near the surface (b); and another prominence produced by the greater trochanter of the femur (c).

Fig. 490. This classical sculpture shows the muscular anatomy of a male figure seen from the front.

488

A   B   C

489

a ▶
b ▶
c ▶
◀ c

Fig. 488. *Contrapposto.* This term describes a typical pose for a standing model, who rests by leaning the weight of the body on one leg, at the same time slightly bending and relaxing the other leg. It is in this position that the pelvis tilts toward one side while the chest and the shoulders tilt toward the other side, and the spinal column twists accordingly.

Fig. 489 (left). This anatomical drawing shows the underlying structure of the hips in the *contrapposto* position. Understanding the interaction of points *a, b, c* is a necessary requirement for drawing the figure accurately.

490

the nude

491

Figs. 491, 492 (above). Francesc Serra, *Nude*. Conté crayon on cream paper (right) Francesc Serra, *Nude*. Gouache and sepia chalk on cream paper. Both drawings were drawn from life in the artist's studio. In the drawing on this page, note the direction of the line and the top lighting. In the drawing on the opposite page, the artist considered the perspective of the background and drew it with a partial backlighting scheme. In both drawings there is a keen sense of underlying structure, based on an accurate calculation of proportions, a knowledge of light, and a surety in the direction of the line.

the clothed figure

Try this exercise: draw several fabrics of different kinds, draped in different positions–on a table, on a chair, or hung on a wall. This exercise will help you solve two major problems: volume and modeling. It will allow you to study the appearance or texture of fabric and to practice shaping of folds and wrinkles which you can apply later when drawing a clothed figure. "Clothes must adapt to the body and never look void inside" (Leonardo). For this exercise you can work with artificial light and choose light-colored fabrics of different textures, such as a cotton sheet, a thick woolen blanket, or a dress of shimmering satin or silk. You should draw on a large piece of paper with charcoal, black chalk, or sanguine. Try to fill in the areas very rapidly, darken them, create whites with the eraser–in a word, paint.

Once you have started drawing clothed models, I advise you to practice the problem of folds and wrinkles. Draw quick sketches from nature. Try to represent wrinkles of a jacket sleeve, made of thin fabric with only a few lines.

Try to understand through drawing how fabrics behave in relation to the body and its movements. Find the point where clothes are more prominent and observe the shaping of creases and wrinkles. Finally, consider the possibility of clothing the figures yourself before drawing them clothed, that is, sketch the nude first with a few strokes, then "dress" the model. This will encourage you to think about the folds and wrinkles as they result from the shape and position of the body.

Fig. 493. The study of fabrics is a good exercise which has been practised by all masters of drawing for its applications to the clothed figure.

Fig. 494. A thin material such as this shirt (A) will have more folds than a thick material such as this coat (B).

Fig. 495. Try sketching a dressed figure, and include the complex creases and folds of one sleeve. For example, A can be drawn by summarizing the folds and B by grasping the nature of the pleats.

Fig. 496. It's a good idea to draw cloth draped on the body, so that you can understand the behavior of cloth in relation to the movements of the body.

493

494 A

495 A

496

B

B

497

Fig. 497. Badia Camps, *Sketches of a Dressed Figure*. Sepia chalk and Conté crayon. Private collection. If you draw the nude frequently, you shouldn't have any trouble drawing the clothed figure.

the canon of the human head

In the *Quattrocento,* Cennino Cennini wrote in his work *Il Libro dell'Arte*, "I'll give you the exact proportions of the man." Incidentally he added: "I'll leave those of the woman, since they are not exact multiples of one another." As if women were different beings! Later on, studying male perfection he added, "The face is divided into three parts, the forehead, the nose, and the area between the nose and the chin."

Cennini established a canon very similar to that on the figure, but applied it to the face. As you can see in the figures below; this canon refers to the height of the head, from the upper outline (without the hair) down to the chin. Observe in Fig. 499 that the canon of an adult head seen frontally (a child's canon is different), is three-and-a-half modules high and two-and-a-half modules wide, the height of the forehead being the module used. (Check these and the following features of the frontal canon in Figs. 499, 500, 501. Notice in these figures too, that the eyebrows, the nose, and the mouth are placed on the vertical center of the canon, whereas the eyes coincide with the horizontal center. Study the placement of the facial elements on the following horizontal lines of the canon:

A) *The upper outline of the skull (leaving out the hair)*
B) *The beginning of the hair*
C) *The placement of the eyebrows*
D) *The placement of the eyes*
E) *The lower part of the nose*
F) *The outline of the lower lip*
G) *The lower outline of the chin*

Notice, too, the height and situation of the ears which coincide with the placement of the eyebrows and the lower part of the nose (module C-E). Finally, see the differences between the canon of an adult head and that of a child in the box on the following page, Figs. 504 and 505. This canon is particularly helpful for drawing and painting heads and portraits. Of course, it cannot be rightly applied to all heads and faces because every one has his or her own unique features. However, there are dimensions and proportions that can be applied in a general way. For instance, the fact that the distance between the two eyes is exactly that of another eye; or that the height and situation of the ears coincide with the distance from the eyebrows to the lower part of the nose; or that the three modules *forehead, nose, nose-chin* are three basic dimensions to be taken into account when starting to draw a head.

Figs. 498 to 501. These illustrations show us the canon that enables us to draw the proportions of a human head, either male or female. Note in Fig. 498 (A, B, C) the construction of the canon through a simple geometric calculation that will enable you to draw a head seen from the front. Study the alignment of the different parts of the head in both a front and side view. In figs. 499 to 501, *A* indicates the top of the head; *B* is the hairline; *C* is the eyebrows; *D* is the eyes; *E* is the lower part of the nose; *F* is the edge of the lower lip; *G* is the bottom of the chin.

502

503

Figs. 504, 505. Head proportions for young children correspond to a different canon than the one used for an adult. A child's forehead is wider; the eyebrows–and not the eyes–coincide with the midpoint of the height of the head; between the eyes is a longer distance than the single-eye distance found in adults; the ears are proportionally larger, and the features are typically shorter and rounder.

506

504

505

Figs. 502, 503, and 506 (above). These drawings were made by Francesc Serra in pencil and blue pastel. Note the difference in the facial proportions between the adults at top and the child's face below.

507

A

B

Fig. 507. As an example of artistic drawing and its expressive possibilities, here are some drawing examples made in the School of Fine Arts of Barcelona in Professor Francesc Crespo's class by his pupils: Joan Sabater (A), María Perelló (B), José Juan Agüera (C), and Raimon Vayreda (opposite page). Permission to reproduce these drawings has been granted by the School of Fine Arts of Barcelona.

C

the art of drawing

What makes a face beautiful is not the brightness of color, it is the perfection of the drawing.

Tiziano Vecellio (1487/90-1576)

the portrait

The two portraits that illustrate these pages are by Francesc Serra, a famous Spanish painter and draftsman who died in 1976. Francesc Serra was a good friend of mine; we published two books together. He was a master of painting oil figures, and a exceptional draftsman in various media as well. These portraits were carried out with Koh-i-noor HB and 2B pencils, on glossy drawing paper. He used a 100-watt tungsten floodlight about two yards away from the model. He would spend between five and seven hours on portraits like these, in one or one-and-a-half hour sessions.

Francesc Serra specialized in lead portraits for a while. "I stopped drawing them," he told me, "because I had too many assignments and I didn't have enough time to paint! . . . Besides, portrait painting is a conditioned type of art: For the artist, the likeness is important, but the drawing as a work of art in itself is even more important. For the person portrayed, it is the likeness above all that counts. The subject expects to see his or her image improved. In the end, you are not free; you have to keep the customer satisfied!"

Serra's idea coincides with the opinion of the sculptor Rodin: "Because of a strange and fatal law, the person who wants a portrait goes against the talent of the artist he (himself) has chosen." But the history of art is not altogether in accordance with this principle. One of Velázquez's best works is the portrait of Pope Innocent X, which is admired every day by hundreds of people at the Gallery Doria in Rome. Nobody remembers if Innocent looked like his portrait, but everyone agrees the picture is a work of art. This is the case with many portraits, including Serra's works.

One of the most famous artists in the art of painting and drawing was Jean-Auguste Dominique Ingres. He left us a series of "pieces of advice for several pupils" which are a superb lesson on portrait painting. Here you have the most relevant items:

• Likeness depends on physiognomy; if you exaggerate the features, you'll come closer to capturing the way a person looks.
• The body does not have to follow the movement of the head.
• Before you begin, get to know your model.
• Remember, eyes are constantly moving; don't draw them as if they were static.
• Avoid an excess of reflections, which might break the massing.

509

The first session of a portrait must be devoted to the study of the pose, the lighting, and the likeness by making several preliminay sketches. The model must be comfortable, clothed naturally, with his or her hair naturally brushed. The model should look at the artist and keep his or her eyes at the height of the artist's eyes.

There are certain fairly standardized measurements for portraits: For a head or half body, a sheet of about 35 × 45 cm (14 × 18 in.) is used; for the whole body, a sheet of about 50 × 70 cm (20 × 28 in.). The size of the head itself should be about 12 to 15 cm (5 to 7 in.); in half body, about 10 to 12 cm (4 to 5 in.); in the whole body, 7 to 9 cm (2 1/2 to 3 in.), Notice that the illustration on the opposite page shows us the classic system: a carefully finished head with light and shade effects with the body sketched in a linear style.

Fig. 509. This portrait in pencil by Francesc Serra contrasts the precise modeling of the head and hands with the linear, sketchy quality of the body. This device also attracts our attention to the model's pose and attitude, which has been studied and emphasized by the artist.

Fig. 510 (right). In this splendid portrait done in lead pencil, artist Francesc Serra has enhanced the magnificent modeling of the head, and indicated the body with just a few confident lines. (This is an example of the classical style of contrasting head and body.) Note that in the areas of the shirt collar, the jacket lapel, the sleeve, and the hand, the use of lines blended with a stump, which is characteristic of Francesc Serra's style.

510

the sketch

A pencil and a piece of paper are all you need for studying, learning, and improving the art of drawing. The paper should be a pad of sheets a bit smaller than this book. The sheets should be bound or stuck together so that you get a stiff surface without using a board. This will allow you to draw anywhere. Use a soft pencil, a 4B or an even softer one, or consider the possibility of using an *all-lead* pencil. A black felt-tipped pen or a set of three or four pens–black, gray, ochre, and sienna, for instance–would be enough. This range of colors allows you to sketch with a slight hint of color.

Subjects can be found everywhere. Remember the famous words by Renoir: "Subjects? Themes? I can do with a pair of buttocks!" All kinds of subjects are valid: trees, seascapes, boats, and a million more. At home, in the street, on a train, in a waiting room, in a hotel. Try spending a morning at the zoo or on a farm sketching animals. As Renoir said, "we can do all right with a pair of hens, three ducks, a rabbit, a cat, and a dog."

Besides being fun, sketches are the best exercise to improve your artistic capability. As Van Gogh used to tell his brother, Théo: "Drawing sketches is like planting seeds in order to get pictures later." Good drawings or paintings are sometimes much better when they are "short." Shortness implies security and spontaneity. When painting a picture, people tend to be scared about the final result. This fear may disappear if you paint as if you were sketching, with the same philosophy, characterized by ease, spontaneity, and freedom.

511

512

Figs. 511, 512. The head and the clothed figure are ideal sketching subjects. Models can be friends or relatives, but they can also be people you can find everywhere: in the park, on a train, or a restaurant. Usually people don't take offense if you ask them to model. However, it's often quite easy to draw people without their noticing.

Fig. 513. The zoo, with its exotic and diverse animals, and country houses or farms, with their variety of domestic ones, offer an inexhaustible supply of fascinating subjects to draw.

Fig. 514. Sketches of landscapes are doubly useful. First you can practice the art of drawing from nature; and second these sketches can provide the raw data for a finished work of art.

the sketch

Francesc Serra shows us six figure sketches here made with pastel and Conté crayon on light cream-colored paper. These sketches were made from nature with quick poses of fifteen minutes each. "Every two or three days, between one picture and the next," Serra told me, "I draw three or four sketches like these, just to keep in good shape." In order to achieve excellent pictures, it is helpful to try this exercise as often as possible.

515

Fig. 515. These sketches of a nude by Francesc Serra are made with pastels and Conté crayon. The studies were limited to poses of five, ten, or fifteen minutes. This time limit obligates the artist to execute the drawing with all its components–line, value, contrast– with extraordinary speed. It also provides an excellent training ground for the artist to synthesize and commit to memory all he or she has learned.

the draft

Helmut Ruheman, chief restorer of the London National Gallery and author of *The Restoration of Paintings* wrote, "I was in Paris working with Maurice Denis for two years. I'll never forget some pieces of advice he gave me. Before starting a picture, draw a quick draft, postcard size. Then sketch the basic composition and the colors, and under no circumstances are you to abandon this small and fresh idea."

In the beginning, the main purpose of drawing was to sketch and project paintings. Many good pictures started as postcard-size drafts. Rubens, for instance, started like that–as can be seen in galleries and museums–with one or two and sometimes three wash sketches with two or more colors, then with one or two oil sketches, which eventually were sent to his workshop (where he worked with van Dyck and Jordaens) to be completed.

The artist Badia Camps shows us here the sketches of an oil painting beginning with a small draft and a more complete drawing. Both of them were made with dark sepia chalk, and a touch of color made also with chalks, to get the final painting. Notice the changes in position, viewpoint, shapes in general, and objects on the table in particular. All this is characteristic of a study carried out with several drafts.

Figs. 516, 517. The artist Badia Camps shows us here the process he followed to achieve this oil sketch he did for the painting on the opposite page. "Sometimes," Camps says, "the idea for a painting starts from a little note such as this drawing." This sketch, eve so small, offers the advantage of allowing you to realize an idea in a minimum span of time– say two or three minutes– by transferring to the paper a synthesis of what you have in mind. Later, this process becomes more laborious, when such radical changes as changing the position of the model are needed for the painting to be resolved (Fig. 517).

516

517

518

Fig. 518. (This reproduction of Badia's drawing is only slightly smaller than the actual drawing.) "Afterward," continues Camps, "you begin the study with gradations of tone and color contrast. I usually make a sketch such as this using pastel on a sheet of white paper about 7 x 9 1/2 in. (18 x 24 cm). Then, I usually leave it until the next day, trying to resolve the rest of the study and perhaps the intended finished piece."

Fig. 519. ...Finally, I make a sketch in oil on cardboard. Then, working with the model, I try to capture in this final sketch all the ideas and concepts stored up from the previous sketches. Two or three days later, I will start the definitive painting." Thus, Badia Camps has shown us here the way to paint a picture successfully, using the same procedure followed by all professional painters.

519

on the art of composition

A young painter named Louis Le Bail had the opportunity of watching Cézanne compose one of his still lifes. Le Bail wrote the following impressions: "He started by taking the tablecloth and putting it on the table. He crumpled it a little bit. Afterwards, he placed the pears and the peaches. He put them on a dish on the tablecloth, next to a jug. He opposed some colors to others, making complementary colors vibrate: greens and reds, the yellow of peaches and the blue of shadows. He raised and inclined the pieces of fruit by putting different kinds of coins under them. He used to do this with great enthusiasm and dedication." Paul Cézanne was a real master in the art of composition. What rules did he apply? None. There are no specific rules in the art of composing. It is a question of creation, of intelligence; and, as the philosopher Jean Guitton says, "intelligence is something that can't be taught, but we can show the right direction to look at in order to see intelligence appear."

The art historian Wölfflin states that "a picture is in debt to other pictures much more than it is to the artist's observation of nature." Therefore, in the first place you should get information: See good pictures by good artists and study their composition. Ingres said, "Beautiful shapes are those in which small details do not question the great masses." This idea may be complemented with Delacroix's advice: "Pay constant attention to the mass, to the image that caught your attention." All this is related to one of the few real rules in the art of composition, stated by Plato in ancient Greece:

*Composing means finding variety
and representing variety within unity.*

Variety occurs in shape, in color, in the position of the elements represented, creating a diversity of shapes and colors that catches the onlooker's attention and makes him interested. But make sure this variety is not so great that it puzzles the onlooker and distracts his attention. In other words, organize this variety harmoniously so that it becomes complementary, and establishes a unity throughout the work.

522

Fig. 522. POOR. This composition is too unified and the placement of the fruit is monotonous and inexpressive; it does not arouse our interest. Note that the attached schematic graphically illustrates the static quality of the composition.

523

Fig. 523. POOR. Here we have an excess diversity of objects. The scattered quality attracts our attention separately; the composition can't be contemplated as a whole.

524

Fig. 524. POOR. Here again we see an excessive unity. As you can see in the schematic, the composition offers far too many geometric coincidences that contradict the natural diversity of things.

525

Fig. 525. GOOD. This composition is a good example of unity within diversity. The unifying factor is the arrangement of the whole, while the diversifying factor is found in the varied positions and arrangements of the objects in the picture.

the law of the golden section

526

Fig. 526. This landscape is an example of how the Golden Section can be applied to achieve the best composition. Let's place the *golden point* in the block formed by the four buildings and the church belfry. You can see that in A the center of the main motif is acceptable, but somewhat monotonous. In B the main motif is displaced toward one side, excessively off-center, to the detriment of a good composition. Finally, in C, the block of the four buildings and the belfry is placed in an optimum situation according to the Golden Section, thus achieving an aesthetically perfect position in the composition.

We know that in the first century B.C. the Roman architect Vitruvius wrote "*De architectura*," which he dedicated to Emperor Augustus. Vitruvius was an expert in painting –he directed the techniques used for the Pompeii wall paintings– and like Plato, he was a theorist of art. While he was working at Pompeii, he studied the organization of shapes and space and wondered about the best place to locate the main subject, the most important element on the wall painting (or picture or drawing). The easiest way, though hardly original, was and still is, to put the main element in the center of the picture. In order to break the excess of symmetry and unity, the center could be taken to one side, but to what extent? Vitruvius found out the solution and established the famous *golden section* or *golden rule*.

"*For an area divided into equal sections to be agreeable and aesthetic, there should be the same relationship between the larger section and the whole, as between the smaller and larger sections.*"

527

The law of the golden section

Let's imagine a segment whose total length is 5 inches.

|← 2 in. →|← 3 in. →|

If we divide this area into two sections of 2 and 3 inches, we will see that, according to the golden section, an approximate proportional relationship exists between the smaller portion (2 in.) and the larger one (3 in.) as

you have 5:3 = 3:2, which when reduced to a decimal fraction gives approximately the same result: 1·6. Vitruvius found this numerical relationship in "*extreme and mean ratio,*" establishing that:

The arithmetical expression of the "Golden Section" is equal to 1.618.

Practically speaking, whenever you want to find the division of the Golden Section, multiply the total length of the space by the

GOLPEN POINT

between the larger section and the entire length (5 in.). Thus-

factor 0.618. Look at the following examples:

foreshortening

Foreshortening is the word used by artists when they wish depict to a body placed obliquely or perpendicularly to our level of vision. Look at the examples and think of all the artists throughout history who have devoted hours and hours to the study of foreshortening, generally as the preliminary step to a real work.

In all foreshortening there is what I call the *two-dimension barrier*. Look at these two hands I drew foreshortened. A sculptor would model these hands with a complete realism, making them corporeal, giving them volume. That's because a sculptor works in three dimensions: height, width, and depth. But we only work in two dimensions: height and width. The third dimension, depth, has to be represented by playing with light and shade effects to create the illusion of volume.

This is no easy task. We are accustomed to seeing bodies in three dimensions. There is a psycho-physical diagram in our brain, which instinctively places some parts of a body at a middle distance in relation to others, which appear in the foreground. Here, too, there is a rule to follow:

We must reduce to two dimensions what we see in three.

Observe three basic factors to achieve that purpose:

1. *See the model without its third dimension.* In other words, see it as a flat object, without relief or foreshortening, or depth. This requires a change in attitude.

2. *Draw objects from nature with low relief.* Begin by drawing faces in profile; go on gradually to three-quarter views (semiprofile) and last, have a try with full-face drawings, with the problem of the nose seen foreshortened.

3. *Try to see the model as shapes or masses.* When you are drawing the nose on a face seen frontally, try to see it as a flat area composed of various values. "Here I have this shape and this intensity, next to it another shape a bit larger, and a light point, a bright area..." as if it were only a sheet of paper showing only two dimensions.

533

Fig. 533. Michelangelo, *The Holy Family*. Crafts Gallery, Florence. All the Renaissance artists showed a special preference for foreshortening, partly, I suspect, because it was a way to show their skill as superb draftsmen. In this picture, note the foreshortened left arm of the Virgin that is shown as a study in figure A.

Figs. 534, 535. Here we can see the foreshortening of two hands, with the index finger pointing forward. To execute this drawing, I drew my own left hand while pointing to myself in a mirror. Why don't you try to draw this particular position? It's a good way to practice.

A

534

535

artistic drawing in practice

Perfect from a starting point, build, search, unite by lines, compare the big distances, the big strokes, harmonize... Drawing is everything, it is art in plenitude.

Jean Auguste Dominique Ingres
(1780-1867)

charcoal, conté crayon, and white pastel

This drawing is by Francesc Crespo (Fig. 546), a friend of mine and an artist, professor and Doctor of Fine Arts and, until recently, vice-dean in the Fine Arts School of the University of Barcelona. He has won several drawing and painting prizes and has had more than twenty exhibitions in Spain and Italy. He draws and paints many subjects but preferably still lifes with pots and vases with flowers, and also nudes. "The human figure is a compulsory subject for me," says Crespo. "I teach two

546

547

Fig. 546 (left). This is Francesc Crespo, the artist who has drawn many of the illustrations for this book. Here, he is showing us how to draw, step by step, a female nude in charcoal and Conté crayon, highlighted with white chalk.

Figs. 547, 548. here we have two samples of Francesc Crespo's art, drawn in charcoal. Both drawings, the figure on the left and the still life below, are quite large, drawn on a sheet of paper 40 in. wide (1 meter).

days a week at the Fine Arts School, and besides studying and preparing my classes, it's a subject I never get tired of." (See Fig. 547, 548 for Professor Crespo's favorite subjects). Crespo's studio is on a top floor with a terrace, two rooms, and a kitchen. It is a working studio, full of boards, folders, stretchers, frames ("I have a fortune in frames"), drawings and paintings completed or half done ("I always work on five or six paintings at once"), three easels, an auxiliary table with drawers and wheels to keep brushes and pencils at hand, a platform for the model in a corner, and a stereo.

The model arrives, goes into the kitchen, and undresses. Crespo turns on the record player. He already has a clear idea about the pose of the model so he starts drawing immediately, while the chorus of *Nabucco* by Verdi can be heard.

Crespo always draws or paints standing up. He does not box up. He goes directly to the con-

548

549

550

Figs. 549, 550. On the left, the drawing in its final stage; the right, the very first lines of the drawing.

Figs. 551, 552. Crespo first draws in the basic structure of the model, laying in the various tonal values, plane by plane.

551

552

tours. He calculates by eye the total dimensions of the model. He uses the charcoal. He marks, he dots in a corner, now to the left, now to the right... He rehearses the stroke before he draws it, swinging his hand from the hip to the thigh. He moves his hand from one side to the other, and suddenly he draws a line, a strong line; he draws it again and stops. He compares model and drawing. He is absorbed and Crespo in drawing with measured, calculated, intense, and secure strokes. His initial drawing shows a solid structure of lines and planes. Another feature of his way of drawing is that when he renders areas in shade, he draws with the charcoal turned in a flat position. He draws and blends with a stump, draws and blends again. But he never completes the blending; it's as if he wanted to leave it half finished. "Why?" I ask him. The answer is definitive. "Because this way, I can keep the idea that all parts are subordinated to the whole work, and that all parts go on at the same time. Blending the shadow of this spine completely would mean that I give it a greater value than the rest of the picture." Crespo begins coloring the drawing with Conté crayon. He draws with a piece approximately 1 in. (3 cm) wide, rubbing softly with the flat side, and using the system mentioned before: draw, blend, stop... draw, blend. He prefers to use his fingers for blending; he rarely uses stumps.

Now he draws with the white pastel, enhancing lights. "Why don't you use white chalk?" I ask. "Pastels are softer, more ductile, and allow a greater speed when drawing and filling in areas." He uses the white pastel as he did the charcoal and the Conté. He limits areas with strokes, as before, he does everything at once,

drawing a nude with lead pencil

559

560

561

562

I mentioned some pages ago that the best way to learn to draw is to draw the nude human figure. Let me add now that if the study of the figure is made with lead pencil the pleasure of drawing from nature is much greater, because of the outstanding possibilities it has to blacken and gray. We will see it drawing this model from nature. I asked her to rehearse some poses, and I chose the one where her back is facing us (Fig. 563). I will use D'Arches glossy paper, a sheet of about 20 × in (50 × cm), with the diameter of the head 2 or 3 in. (7 or 8 cm). I will use all-lead graphite pencils, 3B and 6B, though for the boxing up I will use an HB lead pencil, and a kneaded eraser. As you can see on these pages, the total proportion of the image is almost a square and the structure or basic shape of the model is triangular. The height of the head in relation to the height of the body can be deduced from the canon of the human figure, where, down to the level of the pubis, four heads can fit.

Using the pencil as a system of measurement and imagining vertical and horizontal reference lines, I draw the general structure of the model (Fig. 565). I redraw, erase, and compare until I get a linear drawing that is almost definitive. Then I start graying–without blending–yet trying to keep a certain regularity in my strokes in order to get a uniform blending.

A warning: Graphite is black, greasy, and dirty. You must try to avoid contact between your hands and the paper, and you should wash your hands frequently. Completing the drawing with the paper absolutely clean is expected from any good professional. Another requirement is to prevent perspiration from staining

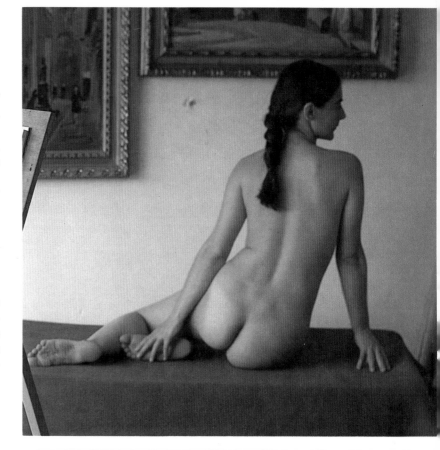

the drawing. Stains due to the perspiration of our hands are invisible at first. However, when there are grays–medium or light grays–the stains become darker than they first appeared and are practically impossible to erase.

In Fig. 571 you can see a half-completed *sfumato* which, as in a half-completed sketch, already hints at the finished drawing. Once this stage has been reached, you should keep in mind the following factor: *Build up values slowly and progressively*, always comparing and being

Figs. 559 to 563. Here you can see the various poses of a professional model. A good model knows the classical positions and does them with an intuitive sense of which poses will make an interesting drawing.

564

565

566

567

568

Fig. 564. Here, the position of the model allows me to box up a triangular shape; and the knowledge of the canon of the human figure enables me to calculate the size of the head in relation to the body.

Fig. 565. The basic structure of the pose is easily resolved with the above mentioned box, but also by following traditional methods, such as measuring with a pencil, and using perspective reference points and lines.

Fig.566. The initial stage of the drawing can be made with an HD lead pencil, which makes very light marks and will go un-noticed later when the tonal gradations are applied.

Fig. 567. Once you have com-pleted the dark shaded areas, you should start using the "all-lead" 3B pencil. By holding it on an angle, you can obtain thick lines that are useful for defining the middle-tone gray areas.

Fig. 568. The dark accents have been drawn in with a certain regularity, so that when they are blended later with a stump, these areas will have a uniform quality.

drawing a nude with lead pencil

571

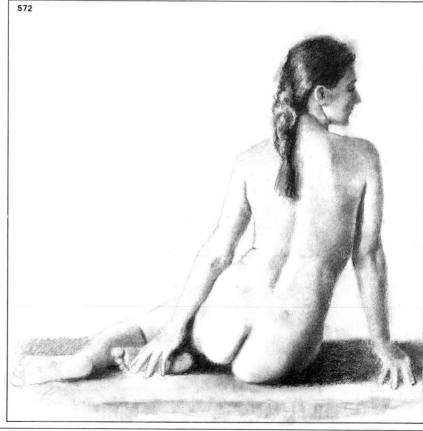

572

careful not to darken too much. Remember that intensifying is easy, whereas lightening is usually more difficult.

Remember that flesh color must be translated into black and white. The most illuminated areas will appear a very light gray. This gray will only be "broken" by the white of a shiny spot, a highlight on the model. Observe this in Figs. 572, 574.

Bodies are soft. Humans are not cold, metallic, or mechanical. Therefore our profiles, our contours, our changes from light to shade must be warm, vague, and soft. You can see this characteristic in the above-mentioned figures. In the final stages of a drawing (Fig. 572), the process of drawing, that is, building value and modeling, must be slow, calculated, and repetitive, especially repetitive in the sense that adding tone and blending needs to be done carefully

573

Fig. 569. Note the sequence used when blending an area with the fingers and a small stump.

Fig. 570. The kneaded eraser can adopt any shape, and this characteristic is what allows us to "draw" with it. In this case, the eraser is responsible for drawing in the highlighted contour of the ear and highlighted areas of the back.

Fig. 571. Blending the areas that create light and shade is often a slow and exacting job, mainly because of the need to build up values.

and slowly, comparing and controlling shapes that sometimes change, because of the addition of a darker tone. Finally, there comes the moment when the final dark accents are added with the 6B all-lead pencil. It is at this final stage when both values and modeling are completed, that the drawing is truly finished.

Fig. 572. Here, the drawing is near completion. A 6B pencil is used to intensify and develop all the range of tones, from the most intense black to an almost imperceptible gray.

Fig. 573. Above is a close-up of the head of the figure. Note the gray tones drawn over the blended areas, which give the drawing a more spontaneous and artistic finish.

Fig. 574. Drawings in lead graphite can be fixed with an aerosol fixative to preserve them indefinitely. However, before you take this last step, it's advisable to wait a few days, keeping the drawing out of sight, as Titian used to do; this way you'll see it fresh and then be able to make any last-minute corrections.

574

portrait with colored pencils

I begin this exercise by drawing three drafts. The first is to study the possibilities of the model posing with a book in her hands, reading. The idea does not work because it simply looks like a human figure reading; it is not a portrait (Fig. 576). I do a second draft. I paint the armchair the color it really is, red. But that does not work either because this red is so deep that it makes me strengthen the colors of the figure, and then it looks like a painting rather than a drawing (Fig. 577).

The third and last draft is the right one: It is clearly a portrait of a woman, it is a drawing, and it is clearly made with colored pencils (Fig. 578).

Fig. 575. This elderly woman, at home in her colorful red armchair, makes an excellent portrait subject.

Figs. 576, 577, 578. The three sketches below are preliminary studies for the final portrait. In the first sketch, the pose is more appropriate for a sketch than for a portrait. In the second one, the intense red of the armchair necessitates a range of intense colors more compatible with painting than with drawing. The last sketch is the most appopiate; the muted tones are suitable for colored pencils and the drawing reveals a sense of the woman's character.

575

576

577

Fig. 579. The portrait begins by indicating the general dimensions of the woman's form.

I begin the portrait using an HB lead pencil, which is much less difficult to erase than colored pencils. I draw in the oval of the model's face, calculating about 4 to 5 in. (10 to 12 cm) high. Using that size, all the while calculating and comparing, the result is the above figure. Next I draw in the features of the face. Ingres said that there is caricature in everything we see. We must try to see the most prominent features of this model, such as the narrow forehead, the white, silvery, spongy hair. The dimensions of the canon of the head may be applied, but not on the forehead, because in this case, the forehead is narrower. Yet the distance between eyebrow and nose, and nose and chin is the same as the canon. The basic concept that "Between eye and eye, there is another eye" works in this case. In speaking of eyes, Ingres said, "Draw the eyes while you are walking," meaning that the eyes must, be drawn separately just as you would draw two eyes that don't belong to the same face. Once the sketch of the head is finished, I redraw the lines of the figure using a *Venetian red* pencil (Fig. 580).

Fig. 580. This stage of the drawing takes into consideration the head and facial features of the model, the dimensions of which are based on the canon of the human head.

580

581

ASSORTMENT OF CUMBERLAND COLORED PENCILS

Face, eyes, hands

Face, eyes, hands

Hair, blouse

Skirt, armchair

Now it is time to paint, but before this, take a look at the chart on this page showing the different colors available in colored pencils (fig. 581). I start on the face with a coat of *burnt sienna*, add a few touches of *magenta* and use *white* for the light on the face. Next I use *dark brown* for the eyebrows and *dark carmine* (almost *black*, as you can see on fig. 582) to outline the eyelids, *ochre* for the iris, *black* for the pupil except the brightness which I paint *white*.

Fig. 582. As is characteristic of colored pencils, the subject is drawn in gradually; values and color are adjusted carefully as the drawing progresses.

582

portrait with colored pencils

I use *black* and *gray blue* for the eyelids. Next, the hair: *ochre-sienna* for the left side and *white* for the lighted areas, a few strokes of *French gray* and *cobalt blue* for the massing of hair. Then I use *burnt sienna* and a little *magenta* for the neck, draw the hands with *dark carmine,* and paint them with *sienna* and *magenta* (Fig. 582). There are two general areas of color in the blouse, warm for the shaded areas and cold for the parts illuminated by daylight. I then use *olive green, dark gray blue* and *dark carmine,* plus *burnt sienna, ochre,* and *bronze* and *silver gray* for the lights (Fig. 582). Next comes the skirt, for which I use *dark gray blue, Prussian blue,* and *black.* I intensify the color of the hands and legs and try a background color for the head using *carmine* for the armchair and a light shading of *cobalt blue* around the profile of head and shoulders (Fig. 583).

583

Figs. 583, 584. In these two pictures, you can see how various areas of the subject progress from one stage to another, especially noticeable in the face and hair areas, which are often difficult. Note also the light and shade effects that make up such complex areas as the woman's dress and hands. The close up of the head is enlarged here almost to actual size. Note that this area is more refined and detailed than are other areas of the drawing.

584

Notice how the red of the armchair makes the colors of the head look lighter, in confirmation of the *Law of simultaneous contrast* (see on page 137 figs. 475 A and B). As a compensation I intensify the colors of the face and also finish up the hair.

The head contains all the colors used in the face (Fig. 583). I reduce the intensity of the background red to obtain a better general contrast. I end up drawing in the elements in the background (Fig. 584).

I finish up the hair almost completely, working its volume, enhancing brightness, and shaping the form. The eyes are finished using *ochre, Venetian red, dark brown*, and *black*. I do addi-

tional work on the eyebrows and eyelids with *purple* and *gray*; and I add a slight touch of *gray* to the eyeballs, on the left side (Fig. 585). Tints of *purple-violet-carmine* are applied to the armchair, *green* for the lamp and *dark brown* for the books, records, and a part of the radio in the background. I paint the shadow under the bookcase a *dark gray-blue* and a *violet-blue*. But I don't sign yet. I will leave that until tomorrow. Then I will look at the finished drawing reflected in mirror, which is a traditional method for discerning any possible errors because it provides a certain degree of objectivity.

Fig. 585. The final result is a fully realized portrait, where the model's person and personality are revealed through the medium of the colored pencil.

drawing-painting with pastels

We are again with Professor Francesc Crespo. Now Crespo will draw and paint a bouquet of wild flowers in a cylindrical white porcelain vase embellished with flowers and blue garlands (Fig. 593).

Crespo uses a white medium-grain Fabriano paper. He has a great deal of pastel colors –more than 150–they are placed on the auxiliary table on the left (Fig. 587). Cool colors are placed to the left and warm colors to the right. In between there is a space where Crespo leaves the colors he uses most often (Fig. 588, 589).

Francesc Crespo's pastel technique is the traditional one. First he boxes up the drawing with soft charcoal: In this regard, he says. "As you know, boxing up with charcoal allows an easy erasing." Then, he redraws and emphasizes profiles and contours with black pastel. He holds the black pastel stick as if it were a pencil. Eventually, he paints with pieces of pastel in a flat position and blends them with his fingers.

Where Crespo differs from other artists is in his way of boxing up and structuring the model.

586

587

588

590

591

592

Figs. 590, 591, 592. Crespo paints with a large palette of pastel colors, working with bits and pieces which he breaks on purpose. When laying in lines of color, Crespo holds the pastel as if it were a pencil; when filling in tonal areas, he holds the stick flat. He also alternates the strokes of color with blending, which he always does with his fingers.

In a few moments, with a few steady strokes in right place, he indicates proportion and general structure, drawing in the model as if it were the easiest thing in the world. You can observe this facility in Fig. 594. Note also the cold tones and dense and mysterious shades of color in the background (Fig. 595).

As for the rest, Crespo's work does not seem very difficult. Seeing him work, one tends to think anybody could do it: He draws in the profiles of the leaves, the petals, and the flowers with black pastel; then he fills in these spaces with various colors.

Fig. 593 (above, right). The model for the pastel still life is a bouquet of anemones placed in a ceramic vase decorated with blue borders.

Figs. 594, 595. In the pastel sketches above, you can see the extraordinary rapidity and confidence with which Francesc Crespo works. These drawings were made in less than five minutes.

drawing-painting with pastels

He lays in the background of leaves behind the flowers, then draws in the blue flowers that embellish the vase. And that is all. But it is not as easy as it appears. Crespo's skill did not appear overnight. "Of course," he says as he goes on working, "I've been drawing and painting for twenty years now!"

Try this demonstration for yourself, noting all the while how Crespo went about completing his drawing. Maybe, once you get started, you won't be able to give it up! This is what I hope for, as I conclude this book.

Fig. 596. Crespo began by painting in the background with a middle tone, so that the flowers can be rendered with darks and lights. Artists typically start working in the largest area.

Fig. 597 (below left). Here, Crespo lays in a dark green behind the flowers. This dark area creates a dramatic contrast against the lighter tones of the flowers and background.

Fig. 598 (below, right). At this stage, the danger of lack of contrast is over. The flowers are highlighted and the whole offers a perfect harmony. "Some people think," Crespo says, "that to create a sensation of spontaneity, it is necessary to leave small unpainted spaces and show the white of the paper." This notion is not always true, however. Too much white space can attract too much of our attention–to the detriment of the painting as a whole.

596

597

599

Fig. 600. Crespo has completed the drawing and there are no white spaces left. The finished work is pleasant, simple, unpretentious-as are the anemones themselves, wild flowers that offer their beauty to whoever wants to look at them.

600

glossary

A

Acrylic paints. Colors made basically of synthetic resins. They began to be used by artists during the 1960s. They are sold in tin tubes as fluid paste similar to oil colors. Acrylics are soluble in water while they are being applied but once they are dry, they become indelible.

Alla prima. Italian expression which means "first time." It refers to the technique of completing a painting in a single session, without any previous preparation.

B

Back lighting. Light that illuminates the model from behind or obliquely, provoking the shading of the places seen by the artist.

Binary colors (Secondary colors). These are purple, green, and orange. Each one is the result of mixing two primary colors.

Borders. A series of drawings, as a *fret,* that frame and surround, another design.

Boxing up. Drawing the basic structure of models by using squares, rectangles, cubes, or rectangular prisms, called boxes.

Burin. A hand tool used for engraving, made of a steel shaft in a wooden handle.

C

Chalks (Pastels). Small cylindrical or square bars of color made of pigments and binding media. Natural chalk is similar to pastel, but more stable and with a harder line. They come in white, black, light and dark sienna, cobalt blue, and ultramarine. Pastels come in many colors.

Charcoal. A thin carbonized willow, linden, plum, or dogwood branch which is used to sketch.

Charcoal pencil. Compressed charcoal encased in wood, giving greater density and blackness than charcoal.

Chiaroscuro. Painting light within shadows to allow the forms of even very dark objects to show. Rembrandt was one of the great masters of chiaroscuro.

Colorism. A painting style that gives more importance to color than tonal value, differentiating forms and volumes only by color.

Complementary colors. Produced by mixing two of the three primary colors. The resulting color is the complement of the third color. For example, purple, mixed from red and blue, is the complement of yellow.

Contrapposto. Italian term used to designate that position of the body that lies in the opposite direction from the rest of the figure.

D

Dry point. Engraving technique using a very hard steel rod with a point of steel, ruby, or diamond to draw directly on a copper plate.

E

"En plein air" painting. Painting outdoors, a way of escaping from academicisms, perhaps because the Impressionists used this expression when they started painting outdoors in opposition to the "official" way of painting learned in fine arts schools or academies. It also indicates the wish of the painter to convey to the onlooker the sensation of being outdoors.

Etching. Engraving made on a metal plate covered with a resinous ground, with a *burin.* Then the plate is bathed in an acid that corrodes the metal of the lines the burin has left without varnish. Once the rest of the varnish is eliminated, you ink the plate and you can imprint the proof.

Encaustics. Pictorial technique consisting of working directly on a wall using colors agglutinated with wax, which are later fixed with a candescent iron tool that makes them unalterable. This technique was used for small mummies' portraits in Egypt.

F

"Fêtes galantes" painting. Paintings that represent the

festive and courtly atmosphere of the French Rococo period. The most representative artist of this genre was the French painter Watteau.

Fixative. Any of several different substances applied to a drawing in order to preserve it against the passage of time, excessive light, and dampness.

Foreshortening. Perspective applied to a single object.

Fret. Ornament made of short straight lines, often intersecting at right angles to form a continuous pattern, as in the swastika ornament of ancient Greek architecture.

G

Glaze. Transparent coat of paint, applied before or over another color that modifies the latter.

Glossy paper. Paper with an almost imperceptible grain, very appropriate for drawing in ink or in lead pencil.

Golden Section. The ancient law of proportion to determine ideal placement of a line or point, aesthetically speaking, within a given space. If the space is represented by line AB, point C should be placed so that CB:AC = AC:AB.

Gouache. A tempera paint similar to watercolor, but with a larger proportion of pigment and with added honey or gum arabic for opaqueness. Gouache is a thick, covering medium, allowing the artist to paint with light colors over darker colors. It dries with a matte pastel finish.

H

Hieratism. A style that's governed by strict rules sanctioned by religion, often used to describe Byzantine art. Monumentality, formality, and rigidity as well as abstraction, characterize hieratic art.

I

Iconoclasm. Heresy of the eighth century that required the destruction of all the painted or sculpted Christian images, since it forbade any figurative representation.

Iconography. Graphic representation of religious images and Christian allegories.

L

Lacquer. A colored substance used in painting. It comes, originally, from a resin produced by some trees in China and Japan.

Lead pencil. A pencil made of cedarwood, with a lead composed of graphite and clay.

Lekythos. Funerary vases from Classical Greece.

Linseed oil. Usually mixed with turpentine and obtained from flax seeds, a solvent for oil paints.

M

Mannerism. Painting from the end of the Renaissance (sixteenth century) described by Vasari as schematic and based on intellectual preconceptions rather than direct observation. Mannerist painting broke the classical rules to heighten drama and emotionalism.

Metalpoint. A lead, silver, or gold point used on a prepared ground to draw black lines slightly less intense than those made by lead pencil. It was commonly used during the Renaissance.

O

Ostracon. Any inscribed fragment of pottery or limestone.

P

Papyrus. Sheets made from a fibrous plant (Cyperus papyrus) in use in Egypt from the fourth century B.C. to A.D. fifth century, when it was replaced by parchment. The sheets were pasted together to form scrolls.

Parchment. Animal skin, generally of ram or goat, treated so that it may be written upon. For centuries, parchment was considered to be

glossary

the best material for works of art, particularly for painting miniatures.

Perspective. The science of graphically representing the effects of distance. We may distinguish between linear perspective, which represents the third dimension (depth) through lines and forms; and aerial perspective, which represents depth using color, shade, and contrast.

Pigment. Any color which, when diluted in a liquid, provides color for painting. Pigments are generally available as powders and may be of organic or inorganic origin.

Pointillism. Drawing or painting with lights and shades using only small dots and sometimes stumping, with a final result similar to a photograph.

Primary. Basic colors of the solar spectrum: red, yellow, and blue.

Priming. A coat of plaster and glue applied to a canvas, cardboard, or wooden board as preparation for an oil painting.

S

Sanguine. A small square chalk bar of a reddish sepia color, similar to a pastel but harder and more compact. Sanguine is also a means of drawing by rubbing or using techniques similar to the ones for charcoals and pastels. Sanguines are also available in pencil form.

Secondary colors. See *Binary colors.*

Sfumato. Italian term for "smoke", meaning Leonardo da Vinci's technique of blending from light to shade "without lines or borders."

Stretcher. A wooden frame on which canvas is mounted.

Stucco. Fine-grained hard plaster made of gypsum and ground marble, used for interiors and relief sculpture since Roman times.

Stump. A pencil-shaped tool with two points, made of spongy paper or chamois skin, used to gray or gradate lines made with charcoals, sanguines, charcoal pencils, chalks, or pastels.

Symmetry. Repetition of the elements of a composition on each side of a central point or axis.

T

Tertiary colors. A series of six *pigment colors* obtained by mixing primary and secondary colors in pairs.

V

Values. Gradations of tones from light to dark.

Vanishing points. In perspective, a single point in the horizon where every parallel line from any direction will converge.

W

Wash. Drawing made with India ink and water, or with one or two watercolors and water. The colors are usually black and sepia, or a dark sepia and a lighter sienna, etc. The paper, the brushes, and other tools, as well as the general techniques, are the same as in watercolor painting. Wash was used by most artists of the Renaissance and the Baroque.

The author wishes to thank the collaboration of the following people and institutions: Vicente Piera for his advice on new drawing materials, Francesc Serra's widow for her kindness in allowing the publication of the late artist's sketches and drawings, Badia Camps for the publication of sketches and studies of the human figure, the students at the School of Fine Arts of the University of Barcelona and the dean of the same school for the publication of several drawings, professor and artist Francesc Crespo for the drawings and illustrations created for the sole purpose of this book.